THE AMER̲ . . . R̲E
COMPL̲ . . . ̲ERSON THAN
CONTEMPORARY VIEWS OF HIM
ALLOW . . .

Significant changes have taken place in the sexual behavior and attitudes of American men. In less than thirty years the suppositions of Sigmund Freud and the findings of Kinsey have been challenged.

from the Introduction to
THE SHANOR STUDY

THE
Sexual
Sensitivity
OF THE
American Male:

The Shanor Study

Karen Shanor, Ph.D.

BALLANTINE BOOKS • NEW YORK

Library of Congress Catalog Card Number: 78-6861

ISBN 0-345-28109-8

This edition published by arrangement with The Dial Press

Manufactured in the United States of America

First Ballantine Books Edition: August 1979

I am in debt to the thousands of men who so generously and openly participated in this two-year study. Their deep concern for the improvement of relations between the sexes was the inspiration behind *The Shanor Study* and its approach.

I would also like to thank Dr. Edgar Robinson, Curtis Hardison, James Shanor, Henry Wood, Dr. Harold Greenwald, Frederick Tutman, Andrew Oerke, Thomas Butler, Mayor Ernest Morial, and Tony Wray for their suggestions regarding content and format of the book, and for their invaluable moral support.

Friends such as Francis and Steven Helvin, James Kelly, Lorraine and William Dorgan, and Carolyn and Robert Mobley facilitated the writing of this book through their encouragement and their generous provision of places of beauty and solitude in which to carry out much of the writing. I thank them.

And finally, I would like to express my gratitude to Juris Jurjevics, Editor-in-Chief of Dial Press, for his critical and persistent part in the creation of this book. His shrewd insight, objective evaluation, and sensitivity to the subject proved a rare and extremely helpful combination.

As a woman writing about men, I felt a special responsibility to represent them fairly and humanistically. All of the men mentioned above assisted me in this endeavor.

This book is dedicated to
Dan Nesbitt
Jim Shanor
Juris Jurjevics
and to all the men
who participated
in this study.

Contents

"I propose a new form of courage of the body; the use of the body not for the development of musclemen, but for the cultivation of sensitivity. This will mean the development of the capacity to listen with the body. It will be, as Nietzsche remarked, a learning to think with the body. It will be a valuing of the body as the means of empathy with others, as expression of the self as a thing of beauty and as a rich source of pleasure.

"Such a view of the body is already emerging in America. . . ."

Rollo May, *The Courage to Create*, p. 18.

Introduction

One's sexual thoughts and experiences are of course very personal. And knowing someone will read these responses—especially someone of the opposite sex—can be embarrassing, exciting, and sexually stimulating. Sharing such information with another person creates its own degree of intimacy, even when done anonymously. As a psychologist and therapist, this situation was not new to me for it is almost impossible to have clients write and speak candidly about their lives and intimate feelings without empathizing and liking something about them.

For two years I conducted a nationwide study of men and sexuality resulting in 4,062 completed questionnaires and seventy intensive interviews with a representative cross section of American men.* This book is an attempt to combine the data from this study to create a dynamic profile of the American male. Rather than

* A sample questionnaire as well as a demographic breakdown of respondents are included in the Appendix.

treating sexuality as an isolated phenomenon, men and sex are discussed within the larger context of individual life-styles, relationships, societal demands, and future possibilities.

The average interview lasted three and a half hours and, of course, centered around very personal subject areas. The seventy interviews were rigorous, and each encounter resulted in considerable information as well as understanding of the interviewee. A person's tendency to be attracted to and feel close to a therapist was coined "transference" by Freud. At times during interviews, a volunteer would try for some type of sexual encounter even though told beforehand, and sometimes reminded firmly during the interview, that no such contact could be permitted. Keeping the situation on a totally professional basis was not only ethically mandatory, but I believe very beneficial. Many men remarked that it was really easier to be completely open and frank with me since they not only trusted my assurance of confidentiality, but also knew they did not have to "perform" sexually or in any way embarrass themselves before me. They even went so far as to comment afterward that they had found it much easier to talk to me about their private sex lives because I was a woman. In fact, they could not imagine confiding, as they had, in another man. Many of the interviewees have kept in touch. Some have come for therapy.

People have asked if I became insensitive to hearing so many people's intimate thoughts. The question has surprised me. How can a person be bored or turned off when another person is trying so desperately to explain a very important part of himself? For that matter, the whole theme of this book is to focus on the richness and holistic nature of these revealing explanations.

Each interview was an experience. In some, the men broke down crying; many other sessions were filled with humor. After the sessions, I received numerous letters and calls elaborating upon previous answers or reporting new fantasies and experiences. One night five gay men sat in my living room discussing their sexual decisions and their futures and asked to come back the next two nights because there was still more to be said. After interviewing a local police officer, I was confronted by a number of his colleagues on the force who requested questionnaires to fill out or formal interviews. I very much appreciated their interest and efforts in this study, but I'm sure people in the neighborhood wondered about the sudden attention I was receiving from "the law."

Then there was the time I answered my phone in the morning to hear one of the interviewees who had not been able to tell me two weeks before whether he opened or closed his eyes during orgasm. "This is Keith." He announced, "I close them!" Click.

Each interview and each questionnaire was different, yet, as I proceeded, some surprising things clearly began to surface from the body of material.

What started as a study of men's sexual fantasies expanded. In hearing the "more total" story of their sexuality and their lives, I reflected upon the flat, one-dimensional, unfeeling attitudes about sex which have been attributed to the American male. As this "hidden" sexuality of men emerged in the course of my work, their sensitivity and feelings became more evident.

A number of them told me that over the years they had felt somehow different from the "normal" male, even strange in some way, because the "locker room" talk didn't quite excite them and even made them feel uncomfortable. They couldn't and didn't enjoy these discussions about the degradation and conquering of women. The men shared their sexual fantasies, discussed their sexual activities, joys, and frustrations. The sessions were often intense and startling. For instance, not one took place without the volunteer saying that he was telling things he had never shared with another person. Other similar remarks: "I was scared to have this interview and wondered how I ever got myself into such a thing. Now I've been talking for three hours and feel like I've only *started* talking about my real sexuality." "It's such a relief. I feel like the dam has burst and so much that I had pent up inside is now flowing."

The time went quickly, as it often does when people are moved. Like William Slattery, who also examined men's sexual fantasies, I often felt a sadness in carrying out this study—a sadness because it's so obvious that both men and women want to feel better about themselves and want to love and be loved by others. As a society, and probably as human beings, we just have been going about it in the wrong ways. At the same time I feel hopeful that things can get better. Perhaps now that we can start admitting to the sexual urges and interests of women, suppressed and denied for centuries, as well as the emotional nature and longing of men, which has been equally suppressed, we can finally start seeing ourselves as persons with great potential for feeling, love, and sensuality—as individuals moving toward being total men men or women—who have the capacity for giving and taking genuinely, without fear or remorse.

Significant changes have taken place in the sexual behavior and attitudes of American men. In less than thirty years the suppositions of Sigmund Freud and the findings of Kinsey have been challenged.

Blaming societally imposed sexual abstinence and ignorance, Freud said that men had to debase their sexual object to attain sexual gratification. This is still true today, but it is not nearly so prevalent as in Freud's time. Men who strongly advocate the double standard continue to see women in a "madonna-prostitute" role and to associate sex with evil lusts.

However, many men are seeing women differently and associating with shared enjoyment, emotional attachment, and essential communication. They love and marry women whom they enjoy being with sexually. They don't frequent prostitutes as routinely as in past years, and if they do, it is only to try the experience, or to have a special act performed which they do not want to share with their regular partner. There are signs that the need for a man to degrade a partner in order to enjoy sex is waning.

Freud also hypothesized that women felt inferior to men because of what he called "penis envy." This supposition has of course been debated for decades. However, largely as a result of the research by Masters and Johnson showing women capable of several orgasms in a short period of time, many men now admit to "multi-orgasm envy." Some in fact are exploring ways to lengthen their own time of sexual enjoyment and improve both the quality and quantity, if you will, of their own orgasms.

Since Kinsey's study of male sexuality in the late 1940s, there have also been significant changes in men's attitudes and sexual behavior. Some examples:

Men masturbate with greater frequency and farther into their adult years. Ninety-seven percent of the men in this study said they had masturbated sometime in their life, close to the 96 percent affirmative response that Kinsey found. In contrast to Kinsey's era, men today do not feel as guilty about it. The activity, although still usually secretively done, is considered to be a more acceptable one. Not only do adolescents masturbate, but so do more single and married adults. No longer simply a substitute for unavailable heterosexual pleasure, masturbation is also used more by all men to relieve tension and as a distinct sexual activity that is quick, pleasurable, and effective. Some men (like women) find they enjoy masturbating even after very fulfilling intercourse just because such self-pleasuring is different. It is often accompanied by fantasies of sexual relations with another. Younger men especially fantasize sex with partners they care for deeply.

Married men masturbate more now than in Kinsey's time, possibly because they no longer view it as a conjugal crime, and because it is a convenient way to have pleasure and relieve tension in the absence of a desired partner. Since not as many men under the age of 35 frequent prostitutes as during Kinsey's time, they may be choosing masturbation over buying sex. Some complain that wives today are too much into their own interests and aren't as dedicated to the happiness of their husbands as they used to be, thereby forcing husbands to masturbate. Whatever the reasons, men of all ages masturbate more frequently, with increased pleasure and less guilt.

Oral sex is much more popular and widely accepted than in Kinsey's time or certainly in Freud's day, when it was considered an unspeakable perversion. Today, it is widely practiced, and in fact has become almost a preoccupation for many males, like a new toy. Men over 35 are more interested in having fellatio performed on them, while younger men enjoy performing cunnilingus on their partner as well.

Anal sex is also much more widely accepted and tried than it used to be. Although not nearly as popular as oral sex, this activity is no longer considered perverted. Heterosexual males are not as hesitant as they once were in expressing their interest in anal sex and no longer consider it an exclusively homosexual activity.

Young men have different interests and outlets. The declining double standard and increasing opportunities for men and women to share interests and time is reflected in the changes in sexual behavior and attitude of the younger male. In contrast to many of his older counterparts who were initiated into sexual relations by a prostitute or a "nonrespected" female, the younger man usually experiences his first intercourse earlier (middle and late teens) with a woman friend. Morton Hunt, who wrote *Sexual Behavior in the 1970's*, refers to the new atmosphere as one of "permissive affection." Young men and women feel free to explore sex and each other as friends first—then as lovers or possible marriage partners. The young male also feels comfortable relating to older women. Similarly, the more independent career woman is finding that a relationship with someone ten to fifteen years her junior can be rewarding and often easier than encounters with men her own age or older who may see her as a threat or not feel comfortable with her life-style and professional success.

Since Masters and Johnson's research and the more general acceptance of the idea of women also enjoying sex has come into vogue, many men have become concerned about their sexual performance. Where procreation, emotional release, and proving sexual powers to other males used to predominate, many men now are worried about their prowess in bed.

What will the woman think? Will he be the best lover she's had? What will she say to others about him? Will she want to make love with him again? Often such concerns get in the way of sexual enjoyment. Exaggerated efforts to "perform" magnificently impede enjoyment. Some people argue that "women's lib," defined as an increased assertiveness of women in all areas, has produced an inordinate number of dysfunctioning heterosexual males as well as an increase in the male homosexual population. Since there are no reliable statistics on how many American males in past years were impotent, did not function sexually as they wanted, or were homosexual, such assumptions are baseless. The larger number alleged may simply be due to a new willingness on the part of men to discuss their sex lives. It is true, however, that the new sexual stance of women and men's concern about performing well produce new problems and can, in the absence of satisfactory solutions, cause retreat or dysfunction on the part of some individuals.

People have recently felt freer to articulate and share their erotic thoughts. Because of new experiences and education through the media, men have more diverse fantasies than they did in Freud's or even Kinsey's time. They (and this is especially true of those under 25) are more tolerant of homosexual thoughts, and more likely to have elaborate, romantic fantasies and a larger number of fantasies generally.

Fantasies center more around fulfilling the partner

and relating to another person than was true in the past. Males feel less guilty about having these thoughts and are finding out that most are quite normal; they can also enjoy many fantasies without feeling or fearing that they have to act upon them. Most importantly, within the last decade, fantasy in general has been seen in a more positive light. People are encouraged to understand themselves through their fantasies and to liven up their sex practices with them. A recent study, for example, showed that men between the ages of 45–55 actually increased their sexual capabilities through enjoyment of sexual fantasies.

Kinsey found that there were several variables which seemed significantly related to a man's* sexual behavior, his attitudes about sex, and his fantasies. While these variables still affect his sexuality, there has been a marked closing of the differential gap among similarly educated groups and among different socioeconomic groups. The blue-collar worker is becoming increasingly like his middle-class counterpart, and both have become more similar to the upper-class male in their sexual interests and behavior, while the male who didn't finish high school is more like the college professor in his sexual inclinations and his tolerance of sexual conduct. Similarity between all these groups is largely due to the media—books, magazines, television programs, movies.

The greatest differences between men center around age, yet even this factor is not as extreme in its effects as it once was. There are still telling differences in the attitudes of the 20-year-old male in contrast to the 50-year-old, due in part to physical capability and magnified by upbringing, historical events, and previous experience. Nonetheless, most men have become more accepting about such activities as premarital intercourse, masturbation, and oral and anal sex. They have enlarged their fantasy lives, and while they may choose not to

---

* His conclusions were confined to the white American male. The variables consisted of such factors as education, socioeconomic status, religious attitudes, and age.

act on them, they are more tolerant than they were toward those who do. There is a present openness, a new respect for individual differences and choices, and an acknowledgment that women are sexual beings as well. But it's difficult to remove all the shackles in a few years, and the older a man is the more restricted he is likely to be. Sometimes he finds himself only masquerading and unable to cope with the radically changing views of himself and sex.

Change is difficult and exciting for all. Each individual responds in his unique way to changes in sexual information and mores. Most men are presently struggling with the dilemmas and crises that such changes bring. But some don't feel any necessity for struggle. Whatever they've decided about their sexual fantasies and behavior (regardless of how sexologists, psychologists, clergy, or peers might evaluate the decision) has brought them personal contentment and happiness; and that's what counts. The actual decision is not so important as its rightness for them; they have found their unique "rightness." These men are not concerned by the struggle of others and wonder why all the hoopla.

Less than half the men in the study said they were sexually satisfied. In general, the older men felt a lack of satisfying sexual outlets and were disturbed by their waning physical capabilities. The younger men have more opportunities for sex, but want to relate more completely. All look more to their marriages and established relationships for sexual satisfaction than did their predecessors.

The media have served an important role in sexual education, the sharing of ideas, and in contributing to these many changes. While men of all ages said they found the pictures in popular sex magazines arousing, and sometimes used them as masturbation aids, they also found the periodicals to be educational and very important in forming their present attitudes about sex. They found many pornographic movies to be helpful in the same way. Interestingly, the consensus was that the heightened sexual arousal a man was alleged to be experiencing during a stag film is a "macho" myth. Although they might find segments of such films arousing, they claimed much of the mechanical explicit sex depicted on screen is not stimulating and is actually often boring. In general, they found the sexually subtle movie to be a greater turn-on.

These men say that they owe a great deal of their liberation and specific education to the media, of which *Playboy* and *Penthouse* are the forerunners. The only element they find lacking is direct discussion in such publications of their sensitivity and capacity for tenderness. This was a common message throughout the study. The American male is a more complete person than contemporary views of him allow.

"To the majority of Americans, sexual liberation thus means the right to enjoy all the parts of the body, the right to employ caresses previously forbidden by civil or religious edict and social tradition and the right to be sensuous and exuberant rather than perfunctory and solemn—but all within the framework of meaningful relationships. Sex, for the great majority of Americans—including the liberated—continues to express loving feelings, or to engender them, or both. It has not been successfully disjoined from love and remade into a simple appetite, except by a tiny minority of swingers."

Morton Hunt, *Sexual Behavior in the 1970's*, p. 38.

1

Orgasm

Male orgasmic response is not as simple or purely physical as it is often represented. Most women do not realize that men also experience different degrees and different types of orgasm.

Men have always said that the feeling of an orgasm can be more intense after a period of abstinence. However, the most influential factor is emotion. If a man is with someone for whom he has strong, deep feelings, and that person is responding with spontaneity and passion, then his climax can be extremely intense. This is in contrast to a perfunctory encounter in which he either feels obligated to come, or is with a person he does not really want to be with, or is somehow feeling hurried or pressed to perform. His orgasm under such conditions generally will be of minimal intensity and even the amount of semen ejaculated will be relatively less.

Perhaps the greater orgasmic intensity in some situations has to do with men discarding the idea of always having to dominate their partners and, in some sense, submitting. That is, submitting to their own feelings and to their partner. This submission, this "letting go" in feeling and lovemaking, is as important for a man as for a woman.

These men who trust to their feelings, who trust their partners, claim that orgasm can be an exceptional and even spiritual experience in its intensity. Women report sensory fantasies during such intense, emotional couplings. So do men. Those who have experienced such "letting-go" orgasms describe them as beautiful and say that they are often accompanied by "cosmic" visions or other sensory fantasies such as "flowing water," "bright colors," and very often great emotional release in the form of bodily contractions and sobbing.

In describing what an orgasm feels like, many men cite variations in orgasmic intensity.

There's a general building up of pressure until it's almost uncomfortable—then I feel a tingling sensation and my body automatically thrusts harder and deeper—almost uncontrollable until all the buildup inside of me is released. It's a very good feeling (differing in intensity—depending on circumstances) and then I have a very relaxed—sometimes exhausted —feeling

•

Just before I come, it's a feeling similar to a sneeze coming on—a buildup and feeling that has to be released. But it's much more enjoyable than sneezing.

•

It's a release, just one big necessary release. That release can come in many degrees and have a variety of feeling, but it is a definite release and a relief when it happens.

•

When you have a rapid sensation through your body of your blood flowing quickly and your body makes rapid motions—and quickness of breath. At the time of orgasm it feels like a great release of tension—

12

and it is as if all your body functions come to an abrupt halt.

•

There are different degrees of orgasm. If you are making love there is one type. If you have oral sex there's a greater degree of feeling than in making love.

•

I prefer oral sex because there's more of an opportunity to see your penis and how the body reacts than when making love—where the penis is hidden. It's like a stag movie. At times watching the woman's body in making love is a turn-on.

•

An orgasm just feels like it's a great physical and emotional release preceded by a tremendous buildup.

•

There are definitely different degrees of orgasm. There are some—in terms of physical matter—that are ejected and how it feels is a standard measurement of how good it was. It depends on how frequently you have an orgasm and how recently. If you have built up a lot of sperm, anxiety, and desire, you get a greater release.

I think the degree of an orgasm depends on: (1) the degree of personal and emotional involvement; (2) response of the partner; (3) how physically compatible you are with your partner—genital size and lubrication; (4) how long it's been since your last sexual release.

•

An orgasm can range from BLAH to a bang-bang, shoot-'em-up delirious almost high feeling. Depends on who you're with.

•

It's always different, never the same. But it's very terminal. When it happens, it's over. Generally the longer it takes to achieve the longer it lasts, and the more intense it is. Generally. Though there are times it happens in thirty seconds and it's so intense it's agonizing.

The partner is responsible for intensity. And the partner can be mental (like fantasizing when masturbating). For me it comes in periods. The drive isn't constant. There're days and weeks with no drives. Then I could have good sex for a week every day in a row.

There's always a loss of consciousness during orgasm. Guess you'd call it dreaming. I'm not aware of what is happening with my partner. I find that if I want to find out what my partner is doing or feeling I have to concentrate. And if I concentrate my orgasm isn't so intense.

•

One degree of orgasm can take you up to a cosmic plane. It depends on your frame of mind during different times of orgasm. I sort of associate the different types with the philosophical Greek words describing time—*chronos*—time that is ticking away—and *kyros*—time filled with meaning. The same differentiation applies to orgasms. There are orgasms that are almost purely physical and focal. Then there are orgasms filled with meaning. The latter can be overwhelming.

A rare few times in life orgasm is an awareness that some other soul is waiting to be born.

•

If I let myself go instead of concentrating on performance, I can have euphoric, sensory orgasms. Grass is an aid to this. Alcohol is a deterrent.

•

It kind of blossoms out. That's what it feels like. I can feel it expelled out into her and wrapping all around us as we thrust toward each other.

•

The sensation is one of pulsing. This builds and finally bursts. It's involuntary from there on.

•

Indescribable. No one is ever going to truly describe it.

•

First you start throbbing. Before I'm inside, if I'm turned on, I start throbbing. This abates when I go in until just before I come when it starts in again. The throbbing takes over and you've gone, flying.

•

For those moments your heart is in your penis.

•

It's poignant, an open, vulnerable feeling as you pass into another human being the stuff of another life.

The answers to whether or not they always experienced orgasm and ejaculation simultaneously proved interesting.

I've had an orgasm without ejaculating. If I've had three or four orgasms already I can once again feel the pleasure of orgasm but not ejaculate. You can reach a stage where you stay hard.

•

I've never had an ejaculation without an orgasm.

•

Ejaculation and orgasm don't always happen simultaneously. Ejaculation is sort of a mechanical act. Orgasm involves both emotional and physical feelings.

•

There's an enormous difference, emotionally and physically, between a controlled orgasm and an involuntary ejaculation. If you're concerned with the woman's orgasm your own is pleasant and satisfying. But it's nothing like really letting go and not modulating it. The latter is simply overwhelming. It's not necessarily better, just different.

Partner and place, and other elements, affect orgasms.

When I'm into Joan having an exceptional climax I'll simply ejaculate afterwards. It's a release but not exactly orgasmic. The times when we come together it's stronger, or when I come alone.

•

Occasionally I'll not be in the mood to ball, and I just come to come.

•

If we've fucked a lot and we're on our fourth, I'll usually ejaculate more than climax.

•

There are nights, days, mornings that I have to get my rocks off. Plain horniness. X-rated movies, separations, romantic dinners get me in a state too. That's when I enjoy quickies. No preliminaries to speak of—flat-out humping.

•

Necking for a long time, or being orally aroused prior to intercourse, results in a very intense desire to fuck. Period.

•

I love quickies standing up. There is something about being weak in the knees and having to concentrate just to stay upright that makes it very exciting.

•

Deserted beaches make me want to ball fast. We'll swim around naked for a while, feel each other up in the water, then stumble ashore and fuck real fast on a sun-warmed boulder.

•

If I've gone for a long while without a woman I tend to have enormous climaxes the first night. Half the time I won't ever realize how powerful it's going to be until it's happening, and then it just sweeps me away, again and again. I'll do it until I think my prick is going to fall off. Being blown is fantastic then because my cock is so sensitive after all that fucking.

•

Every business trip ends up with my returning home with straightforward lust in mind. My wife is used to it and kids me about it when I'm leaving. She follows up by teasing me when I call home. So I'll race home from the airport and right into bed. Those are very special, orgiastic, delightful sexual encounters. Almost worth leaving home.

•

I fucked for three days straight when I got out of the Army. The poor broad gave out the second night. I wanted more and went out and picked up a Chinese chick and went at it for another day and night.

•

Balling is basic. To really get off, though, there's nothing like a blow job. I don't mean somewhere in a doorway. I mean going down on somebody you really care for and her doing at the same time. Trying to time it makes you wild after a while. The sounds get to me also. It's primitive and your ass feels like it's falling off, and when one of you comes it triggers the other. Frenzy, man.

•

Taking her from behind blows me away. It's not like face to face. When you thrust forward is when it's good. From the back it's the opposite: it hits you as you pull back.

•

Listen, three hours of balling and I don't know where my penis begins and her cunt ends. It gets hard to know whether you've come or not. It feels like you have but afterward I'll still be hard and maybe come again or lose it.

•

I've had sex without physically ejaculating yet in every other respect I feel as though I had experienced exactly that.

•

Dry-humping—doing it with your clothes on—I'll climax but not ejaculate.

•

When my girlfriend has me come in her mouth I'm not completely certain that I've ejaculated. The tactile effects are too confusing for me to tell. I know I've climaxed but did I really discharge sperm? She always says yes, yet I'll not be sure.

•

I'm married, have two kids, a very good marriage and a sexy, affectionate, spunky mate. I also have a sometime male lover whom I don't plan to give up. It's too good with him. The duality is so appealing. He knows, he follows my every reaction. No woman could, of course. We have the same bodies, he and I. It's another type of orgasm and ineffable in its tranquility and intensity. I love my wife. However, I don't intend to deny myself the experience of another man.

•

Prolonged intercourse, caressing, etc., builds me up to such a state that I am fully cognizant of every sensual nuance, and at the same moment I feel drowsy, floating outside myself. My orgasm eventually brings me back temporarily. After coming I drift out again. Usually there is very little verbal communication. That's one of the signs. It's just unnecessary and intrusive.

•

I trained my dog to lick me to the point of my coming. It took me months to get over how strong it was. Thank God she can't talk. I still find it somewhat shameful.

•

If Wendy holds her fingers, like a ring, around the base of my penis I experience the most pleasurable orgasms. She actually did it to help stimulate herself; her clitoris is high up. But it worked on me also. It may be a psychological thing; I think it is.

It defines, gives evidence of my penis being where it is and connects us. The effect is very euphoric and heightens my orgasm immensely.

•

I had a great orgasm by accident several years ago and since then like to have my partner duplicate this. The woman I was with had an electric vibrator and wanted to come by putting it on top of her clitoris while I had my penis inside of her. Very soon I realized that this was very exciting for me, too. The vibration was exceptionally stimulating. After my partner had her orgasm, I stayed inside without moving. Very soon the vibration made me have an uncontrollable and intense orgasm. Who says only women can enjoy vibrators?

During orgasm some men experience sensory fantasies:

Images of light and space, movement. Light (blues, green, yellows, purples, whites) in cool darkness, clean and clear; flowing easy-fast movements of tremendous grace and power; beautiful forms of light moving through space.

•

Wind, sand, breezes, clouds. Music very difficult to hear but demanding to be heard because of its beauty.

•

Water, rain, streams (near and small and quick). Water from the ocean, cool deep pools (dark).

•

A beautiful woman dancing a tremendous dance that is everywhere and forever.

•

There is a feeling of no weight yet moving very fast with bright star clusters all around. We move together, two humans being a creature we cannot be while alone. Sometimes we move inside tubes, sometimes in black space. The fantasy begins and ends with eye contact with the woman. In between the creature we create is like two humans joined at the pelvis, or two bright multicolored flowers from the same stem undulating in a pulsing breeze. I come out of the fantasy near orgasm, then go back into the fantasy afterwards with everything the same except for the feeling of speed.

Often I experience extreme euphoria and feel as if mind is detached from body. Sometimes fantasize being outdoors in wooded-grassy glen.

When their orgasm is over some men pull away while others want to prolong the intimacy:

After orgasm I just want to rest, rest, rest.

•

I suddenly come back to reality. If I'm with a woman I want to be with, I want to touch and hold her. I like it if she massages me or gently scratches my back and I do the same to her. If I'm with someone I'm not really into, I feel like leaving—like pulling away from her and either turning over and going to sleep or just packing up and going home. Sounds kind of cold—but the person I'm with makes a big difference not only to how good—or complete—the orgasm is, but also to what I want to do after.

•

When I have an intense orgasm with someone I care very much for, I suddenly feel very vulnerable. I want to be held—to be close—to be loved—to be assured. Sometimes I almost feel a little afraid, not of that person, of course, but of life and the bigness of things and the littleness of me in this universe. Sometimes I feel like crying, like being a little boy again, and being held by my mother or someone else who will love and protect me.

•

After orgasm I have this uncontrollable urge to get up, light a cigarette, and just sit in bed smoking, pondering, but not thinking about anything in particular. I don't feel like talking. I don't feel like cuddling (and this upsets my wife). I don't feel like doing anything but staring blankly into space and smoking my cigarette.

•

After I have an orgasm I feel like talking and philosophizing with my partner. That's why I always go to bed with women I am into and can share ideas with as well as my body. It's as if my creativity starts flowing at this time and I enjoy "creating" with the woman I'm with. If we have sex during the daytime —it can almost be invigorating. My blood is flowing and I feel really alive. Sometimes I can't wait to get to pencil and paper and writing down my new ideas.

•

The way I feel after orgasm is as varied as the partner I'm with, my mood and physical condition before orgasm, and what I have to do or don't have to do after.

•

After orgasm I'm very hungry—usually want something with some salt in it. I'm also rather thirsty at times.

As enjoyable as orgasm can be, it's not always the most crucial part of a sexual encounter:

Having orgasms is not as important as it used to be —maybe because I am not deprived sexually, and if for some reason I don't come one night or two with a woman, I feel I can get into another situation where I can come—or even go and masturbate. More important to have pleasure and general enjoyment with the other person.

•

Yes, it's quite important. But it's not difficult for me to have an orgasm. My biggest concern is fulfilling my partner. I can always have an orgasm after she's had hers.

•

Having an orgasm isn't necessarily top priority. The whole sexual act and communication and feeling with my partner take precedence.

•

Having an orgasm is superimportant only if I am especially horny. Then I really want to get my rocks off. After the first orgasm I'm more concerned about getting hard again to prolong sexual activity with my partner than necessarily having an orgasm.

•

It depends on who I'm with. If I respect and love the girl it wouldn't kill me if I couldn't come for some reason. But if I'm paying to get head or to have an orgasm, I sure as hell expect to have my partner do what she can to make this happen.

•

Generally no. But I went through a situation where I was concentrating so hard on giving my girlfriends multiple orgasms that I wasn't able to come when I was ready. That bothered me because I needed the release, but couldn't do it. It was so embarrassing.

•

Yes, I feel like I have an orgasm "coming to me"— so to speak—after I've given my partner extensive foreplay and her orgasm. Isn't that why I'm in bed in the first place, to get an orgasm?

•

There are many parts to sex. And although I enjoy having an orgasm, there are many other things I enjoy about sex. I enjoy relating to my partner. I enjoy our touching, caressing, massaging each other. I can get pretty lonely at times—and although I can always masturbate to get an orgasm, I can't always find a tender, interesting partner to enjoy myself with. I enjoy being with someone I can learn from and who can learn from me. Exploring and creativity in sex is important to me. If I have an affectionate and exciting time with a special person—I would not feel especially deprived if for some reason I couldn't have an orgasm. There are few things as exciting, by the way, as knowing you are an important part of an intense orgasm that a woman's experiencing. To watch the look on her face, hear her screaming, or feel her thrashing about is almost as good as having my own orgasm.

FAKING ORGASM

For years women have discussed and gone through the dilemma of whether to "fake it" or not. Many decided to do so in order to preserve the man's ego. They might fake it if, after constantly trying, they can't get theirs. If they do feign an orgasm well, their man can have his and they can get on with sleep.

Did she or didn't she—the debate of the ages. Guess what? Men also fake it. They do especially as sexual relations have become a more equal experience than in the past when the man opened his uninterested wife's legs and simply released his weekly orgasm. Now many men feel that if for some reason they can't orgasm, their partner will assume something is wrong with her and that her ego will be injured. Out of consideration for her, he'll do a bit of staging himself. Or if his partner seems to be fulfilled and he is not able to orgasm he may pretend, so they can settle down for the night.

How can a man fake an orgasm? Not so difficult for a woman to do, but a man? Except for the evidence of ejaculated semen, it's not difficult for a man either. Different men give off different amounts of semen and the same man also varies in this from orgasm to orgasm. Women know this. And when a man is deep inside, it's not always possible to know if he has indeed ejaculated. Especially after he has already had a previous orgasm and she is still very wet inside. The new amount of wetness is not always calculable (since much of the faking does take place after the man has already climaxed once), so it is not so difficult to fake. The man just imitates the motions of his "usual" orgasm. If, as orgasm begins, he usually thrusts faster and harder into his partner, he will do that. If he usually pants harder, groans, moans, or makes other utterances, he will do that. He can even vaguely simulate the post-orgasmic throbbing of his penis and hope the proper unsexy thoughts will quickly return his penis to its flaccid state.

An astute, experienced woman might still be able to tell the difference or may at least suspect. But why does it matter one way or another? The more important issue at hand is the same one we have been dealing with for years. The big problem between men and women is the pressure to perform and the lack of communication. Yes, men too indulge in simulating orgasms in order to preserve the woman's pride and/or simply to complete their performance.

Fake it? . . . Amazing. I never thought I'd ever be asked. Ah, yes. Yes I have. In fact, it's not unusual at all for me. I mean, when I'm fatigued and she's not, I have fucked without actually coming. No big deal.

•

Funny you should ask. I have wondered myself if I do fake it or not. Especially after having come once or twice it's pretty hard to tell. Also, there are times when you concentrate on the other person's coming so much that your own climax is nearly forgotten and seems somewhat secondary. Occasionally I'm so curious to see her come that I kind of forget, too.

•

Men fake orgasms sometimes. It's not difficult to do. When you can't reach it what else are you going to do? You know an orgasm can be unattainable sometimes for a man. Excruciatingly unattainable.

•

Yes, I have faked it. It's not difficult. Contrary to the convenient myth that the aroused male's penis will turn blue with pain and fall off if coupling isn't consummated by ejaculation, the male member will simply subside if one doesn't come.

•

I think almost every man fakes an orgasm at one time or another—he just does it by going through the same motions of a real orgasm—except of course he doesn't ejaculate.

•

I sometimes fake an orgasm—usually so the woman won't think something's wrong with her. It's usually after I've come once already. So she's still wet and probably doesn't know the difference.

2

Masturbation

Although deprecated for many years, masturbation is now recognized as a positive normal activity which can be used to enhance self-awareness and eroticize intimacy with another person.

In addition to orgasmic outlet in sexual relations, it is a popular form of sexual release and enjoyment.

The *Kinsey Report* showed that almost all males masturbate at some time in their lives. Subsequent public discussion about masturbation and articles in popular men's sex magazines helped change the prevailing negative attitudes toward this otherwise "normal" sexual outlet. A majority of men, especially among the white middle class, are more accepting of masturbation as a result.

How many men in the study said they have masturbated? And of those who do, what are the statistics relating to this activity? My findings are not unlike Kinsey's almost thirty-seven years ago. The only difference is that men of all socioeconomic groups say they masturbate more. This is probably due to the relaxing of taboos against male masturbation over the years. Four percent of the men in my study said they had never experienced masturbation (one qualified this by saying he had never been able to masturbate toward orgasm). Two percent said that although they have experienced it, they never masturbate anymore, and 11 percent said they "almost never" do; 16 percent say their activity averages once a month, while 22 percent of the men say they engage in this activity about once every two weeks and 28 percent several times a week. Finally, 9 percent of the men questioned said they masturbate daily and 8 percent say they do so several times a day.

This last group said they think about sex often (more than the average) and report great variety in their fantasies. The men in this group are from varied backgrounds and age groups (all are under 55). However, their ethnic root is "Caucasian" and almost all are unmarried. Though given to masturbating frequently, almost half of these respondents claim they are sexually satisfied.

Like Kinsey, I found that the younger men below the age of 24 generally masturbate with the greatest frequency. However, it is not uncommon for highly motivated, energetic, successful, and charismatic male professionals—i.e., the overachievers—to masturbate daily, regardless of their marital status or opportunities for sexual relations. These men seem to have a great deal of energy and creative tension which is also sexually arousing and seeks sexual expression.

I masturbate infrequently, but when I do, it's usually related to some pleasurable sexual experience that I have previously experienced.

•

I only masturbate when my sex life is lacking. I think of some woman I want to have sex with and what we might do. Women with big breasts and blond hair turn me on.

•

Masturbation, yes, it's a good tension releaser. Not as good or as thorough as an orgasm with a woman that I really want to be with, but masturbation certainly has its function.

•

When I'm busy and don't have time for even a noon quickie, I go in the bathroom and masturbate. It relieves the tensions.

•

I always say, a good fantasy is better than a bad fuck. If I don't feel like being with someone else or if I'm not into the women around, I will go home and have a good ol' fantasy and a fun time masturbating. No hassles. I can go at my own pace, and I know what feels good to me. I can think of what I want or read some some sexy story or look at some arousing pictures. Then I can collapse and go into a restful sleep, without being rude to anyone.

Some men masturbate while reading a sexually arousing book, looking at pictures, or even watching a TV program. Others find arousal through autoeroticism—watching and being turned on to their own body—especially the erect penis. Fantasy is often used to facilitate many men's masturbatory activities, and the fantasy is usually about sex with another person. Of course, a man isn't hooked into any one approach and might use a magazine picture one time and a fantasy the next.

I enjoy masturbating while watching beauty contests on TV or flipping through magazines like *Playboy*, etc. I fantasize going to bed with the women I'm observing.

•

I might masturbate to a sexy book or magazine.

•

29

Masturbation to me is a convenient way of having pleasure. When I fantasize ejaculation takes place very rapidly.

•

I imagine I'm jerking off in front of assorted witnesses.

•

When I masturbate I usually fantasize about certain women I would like to seduce or about my relationship at the time.

Those who use external stimuli, especially visual aids to arouse them in masturbation, keep their eyes open during most of the activity while the fantasizers close their eyes most of the time.

Autoeroticism may provide arousal during all of masturbation for some men while others open their eyes during orgasm to enjoy the sight of ejaculation.

I turn myself on to myself—my desire to touch myself, feel sexy and sensual and sometimes (most times) proceed in order to ejaculate.

•

It turns me on to watch my penis as I masturbate. It is so hard and strong. I like to watch my hand expertly and quickly move the skin up and down. Finally there's a fountain explosion of semen—a turn-on in itself.

•

In masturbation, it's thrilling to watch the sperm spurt out when I come. I have a contest with myself to see how much sperm will come out and how high it'll go. If I don't have sex for a while, the velocity and amount of sperm seems to increase. The sperm shoots the highest with the intensity of the orgasm. If I'm really tired and not in such great physical condition, the sperm doesn't go as high. But when

I'm feeling very randy and in perky condition, it'll really spurt out there.

•

It's a turn-on to watch myself masturbating, especially when the white semen comes gushing out. That's one thing you can't enjoy seeing in intercourse. In masturbating, I really get turned on to myself.

Autoeroticism is not uncommon among women— many of whom are turned on by the touch and sight of their bodies just as men are. With women the turn-on is more to their whole body, especially their breasts and genital area—with men the turn-on is usually focused on the penis and its activity.

The men in the study told of a variety of masturbation techniques. Here are some examples:

I take my right hand and get a rhythm motion going up and down—moving the loose skin and touching the fringe area around the head. Sometimes I put lotion on my hand to lessen the friction. I start out slowly and go faster and faster. I can feel my penis swell in my hand—then the sperm comes exploding out.

•

I lightly play with the head of my penis and around the edges of the head—before I really start moving the skin up and down. The head is especially sensitive and arouses me a lot. Then I grab the stem and work it up and down until I come.

•

I masturbate by holding and rubbing my balls with my left hand as I get the up and down action going on my penis with my right hand. My balls are very sensitive to touch and playing with them and moving them up and down stimulate my orgasm. (This is also true—I like to have my partner play with my balls before and during orgasm.)

•

When I was a kid I used to masturbate into a silk handkerchief so I could wash it immediately after. I still use such a handkerchief or scarf—and find it is a real turn-on. Makes the feeling better.

•

To provide masturbation variety, I sometimes use a cored-out apple or a grapefruit with a hole cut out of it. I don't do this always, but it does feel good. That is if the fruit is room temperature or warmer. Out of the refrigerator might have the opposite effect. OOooh!

•

A ripe melon can be a good masturbating aid. Honeydews and watermelons are good. When in the Caribbean, I tried a papaya and that was pleasurable too.

•

When my wife and I can't have intercourse for some reason (like when she was very pregnant), she accommodates my masturbation by greasing her thighs with cooking oil or coconut oil. I slip my penis in and she squeezes her thighs together and I move in and out till I come.

•

Learned this from my wife. I masturbate by using a vibrator. First I put the vibrator very lightly around the head of my penis. It's very arousing, but I can't really put it square on the head, because the feeling is too intense.

•

I learned this technique in the fraternity house, where experimentation among horny students is common. We used an empty topless can with the sharp edges smoothed down. Then we'd put a nice fresh piece of liver in the can. Felt just like a pussy. I still use this technique to masturbate or else just use a piece of very tender meat which I wrap around my dick. Of course, then I use the regular masturbation movements to come.

•

I masturbate by moving my penis up and down between my wife's voluptuous breasts.

•

I have a long stick hooked to the ceiling. On it I hook a soft leather noose into which I insert my erect penis. When I lie flat on the bed the noose is near the top of my penis. When I arch my back and put my hips up the noose comes down near the base. I then move my body up and down and the noose brings me to orgasm. It's exciting to watch this. In fact, I have a mirror on my wall to add to the visual delight. The whole thing is great for a novel feeling. Also, my hands are free to do other things. Usually I play with my balls with one hand and rub or pull on my nipples with the other. I've used this technique for several years and find that my pleasure increases as I get more practice.

•

One of the various techniques I use as a change of pace is this. I lie flat on my back and bring my legs up near my chest. I put my penis between my thighs. When I squeeze my legs together the sensation is fantastic. By squeezing my thighs together and rocking my body back and forth, I can induce an exhilarating orgasm.

Some men wish they could masturbate by fellating themselves. If only their penis would reach their mouth—or vice versa—they envision a wonderful time. Some very limber and lithe individuals have indeed accomplished this highly desired feat. A number of men try to simulate this feeling by using a warm wet substance in their hand. Vacuum cleaners are used to get the sucking feeling. Never underestimate the ingenuity of a sexually aroused male.

There are even different stances sometimes reflecting

cultural differences. Most American men prefer to lie down on the bed or somewhere when they masturbate. Europeans that I asked say they prefer standing. One Swedish man offered that regardless of his frequency of intercourse, he enjoys masturbating once a day. He does so by standing in front of the toilet—bracing himself against the wall behind the toilet with his left hand and masturbating with his right hand. "I prefer this technique," he says, "it's the way I started and is still my favorite." Many Middle Eastern or Asian men like to masturbate as they squat with both feet flat on the ground.

While many men enjoy masturbating, some do it only to relieve tensions and as an unsatisfactory substitution for intercourse.

Masturbation is often the best of all evils. I'd much rather be with a woman I want to be with and making love. But if this isn't possible, masturbation at least gets me through the day, or the night.

•

I really don't enjoy masturbating very much. Feel kind of deprived and angry when I have to do it. Would like to have other alternatives. But when something's got to be done . . .

•

I like to masturbate. It's just another way of getting sexual pleasure and one in which I am in full control. I can relive in my mind any good experience I've had while I masturbate or fantasize all the many things I'd like to do. This way my opportunities are limitless, at least in fantasy.

Some who do enjoy masturbating share this activity with their partners. Mutual masturbation can enhance a relationship. This may happen in a sexual relationship or miles away from a desired partner. When a man's physical capabilities are waning, use of vibrators, oral sex, and masturbating a woman can fulfill her and build up to dual orgasm in intercourse.

When I'm traveling, I usually call my wife at night before going to sleep. Often at the end of our conversation we'll arouse each other verbally and masturbate ourselves as we talk. That's called "long-distance sex."

•

It took me a while to get enough nerve to do this but when I was with the right girl we decided to masturbate together. Actually she masturbated first for me. It was a great turn-on and she suggested—after she rested a bit—that we masturbate together saying to watch me would be a turn-on for her, too.

•

It is an intimate feeling to share masturbation with the woman I love. More intimate and personal than intercourse. We feel we are sharing one of our deepest and longest secrets with each other.

•

Mutual masturbation is an exciting way to stimulate oneself and one's partner at the same time. It adds variety to a sexual relationship and sometimes is a necessary form of sexual outlet when two people can't have intercourse for whatever reason.

•

When my wife and I masturbate together it is very enjoyable. Not only that, we learn very practical ways to please each other so we can mutually manipulate and masturbate each other. Or when I watch her masturbate, I see how and where she places her fingers. I see how her body moves and get a sense of the timing that is good for her to get off. They say a picture is worth a thousand words. Well, when I watch her in action, I know more than a thousand of her words could tell me. She says the same about how she's learned to please me by seeing how I please myself.

"It is easier in our society to be naked physically than to be naked psychologically or spiritually—easier to share our body than to share our fantasies, hopes, fears, and aspirations, which are felt to be more personal and the sharing of which is experienced as making us more vulnerable."

Rollo May, *The Courage to Create*, p. 15.

3

Fantasy Power

Fantasy is a powerful force in all of our lives. Through our imaginings we examine and explore and we plan for our lives. We create. In realizing and understanding our fantasies, we can better understand ourselves and that which we fear or desire. Whether we choose to carry out our fantasies or not, fantasizing can release fears and desires. They are self-stimulations and mock-ups of our options. In fact, deciding which fantasy to carry out is actually a decision about the kind of life we want to lead, what roles we choose to follow, which style of living we fashion for ourselves.

Sexual fantasies are as diverse as the people who have them. Until recently these deep personal secrets were not explored or shared by people. And in intimate communication between individuals, the physical elements took precedence, but thoughts were masked and often misunderstood. It is still not uncommon for two people to expose their bodies to each other, to join in sex and yet not disclose their feelings.

Further, many individuals worry about their sexual fantasies, thinking them perverse. This of course contributes to self-isolation, chastisement, and occasional impotence. Fears of even having sexual thoughts sometimes lead to emotional disturbance and irrational, and perhaps dangerous, behavior. Impulses, imagined situations suppressed by the individual sometimes explode into behavioral outbursts such as rape, exhibitionism, extreme sadomasochism. If sexual fantasies could be recognized, understood, and somehow released either in sharing, acting out, or just plain allowing oneself to have these thoughts, such uncontrollable consequences could be avoided.

Fantasies are dynamic, changing as we change. A sexual thought that turned us on at 10 years of age won't necessarily cause any arousal when we are 15 or 40. As we have new experiences, read new books, see movies, we add to our store of fantasies. And as long as we don't actively try to suppress any of these sexual thoughts, we can choose and nurture the types of fantasies that we'd like to have. By understanding ourselves and taking responsibility for our lives and our sexuality we can control our fantasies rather than be controlled by them.

Fantasizing can be fun. And our sexual fantasies can be tools for gaining new insights.

Until recently women's sexual fantasies were an especially well-kept secret. Although the popular double-standard puritanical view was that females rarely thought about or enjoyed sex, sexologists of the last century such as Krafft-Ebing, Freud, and Kinsey reported women as having an abundance of such fantasies. It was not known precisely what these fantasies really were; however, this lack of knowledge about women's sexuality encouraged a general attitude that women were mysterious, unpredictable creatures and often fostered an unnatural antagonism between the sexes. At the same time women didn't know what other women were thinking about sex, and in those days of "good girls" and "bad girls" those who endeavored to stay in the "good girl" category worried unnecessarily about the "bad girl" fantasies that commonly popped into their minds. So they built protective facades while often feeling guilty and worried about the unspeakable thoughts they harbored. With men the situation was different, but often no better.

Art and literature through the ages have been concerned with men's sexual fantasies; men fantasizing was condoned and accepted. Even so, fantasies different from the acceptable kinds produced guilt and anxiety in the less restricted male mind. What if his fantasies went farther or were different from those celebrated by pin-ups or *Playboy* center folds? Did that mean that he was not a real man? Many worried unnecessarily. Many more felt that the important elements of caring and communication were missing from the American stereotype of masculinity. Their private fantasies often replaced these missing emotional parts, but many men felt they were alone in these longings.

The media of recent years have done a great service in educating people about sexual possibilities and allaying many fears about perversity in thought and action. But magazines and movies have not gone far enough to incorporate men's longing to love and be loved. They still monolithically treat men like the tough, unfeeling stereotype who is aroused by some visual stimulus—some beautiful and sexy woman, "some good piece of ass"—and who then acts sexually in mechanical fashion. This stereotype has done a great disservice to both men and women by ignoring and denying and denigrating the sensitivity that is also present in the male.

This sensitivity is evident in men's sexual fantasies. So are many other qualities, such as the sincere desire to fulfill their partners. Their fantasies reveal very individual ways which each wishes to experience himself, to experience his own sensitivity.

Fantasies present profiles of what is important to a

person in many aspects of life. The following are examples of such sexual imaginings.

THE TOP TEN

Influenced by his experiences, as well as his attitudes about himself and his sexuality, the types of fantasies a man has reflect his cultural heritage, his learning, and his values. But neither men nor women are tied to their fantasies. They can bring in new fantasies, discard old ones, and nurture and enjoy the ones they like.

Some of the fantasy types which are more popular among some age groups than others have been discussed. For example, men 40 years old and over have the most fantasies about sex with prostitutes. These same men have fantasies involving younger women, while men in their teens and 20s frequently imagine themselves with older women.

Sensory fantasies during orgasm are most prevalent among the younger groups, but power and achievement fantasies (although enjoyed more by men in their late 30s and 40s) are common to men of all age groups, and reflect the achievement-competition values men are inculcated with from childhood.

The following fantasies rank among the "Top Ten" among all contemporary American men:

1. The Nude (or Seminude) Female Body

When I masturbate I think of a naked seductive woman with large breasts and a beautiful cunt.

2. Sex with a Woman Not Previously Involved With

Masturbatory fantasies usually involve a woman I have not had sexual relations with. Generally I "set up" the fantasy by pretending that the woman is attracted to me and picks me up. Usually the love-making positions are varied. I don't get fellated too often in my fantasies. Usually it's just straight fucking.

•

A girl runs into my office, closes the door behind her, rips off her clothes, and begs me to have intercourse with her. After I succumb she then wants to fellate me and I willingly consent.

•

Seducing women I have known in the past usually takes place just before falling to sleep for the night or just after waking in the morning. Usually my fantasy finds me either in bed with these women or outside in some beautiful park and the like. The love-making imagery always involves quite a good deal of mutual pleasure and is rarely bizarre—just two people making love ardently. My women lovers have long hair, attractive figures with large breasts (none of them have braces). My sexual feelings are almost always accompanied with feelings of "real" love, i.e., it isn't just a sexual seduction scene. The women are not strangers. The specific sex activities are standard face to face, oral/anal, etc. Fantasies like these are almost daily occurrences but change from one woman to another. They are rarely replays and I certainly would appreciate an opportunity to test out my imagination.

3. Sexual Replays

If I've had an especially good sexual experience with someone I often think of it again to arouse me during masturbation. For example, a couple of months ago in Tahoe I met a beautiful, sensitive woman. She enjoyed making love so much that the expression on her face and the sounds she made were terrifically exciting to me, so I think back on our time together.

4. Sex with Two or More Women (Including a Mother-Daughter Team)

The masturbatory fantasy is usually some visualization of a past sexual encounter or a group sex scene where I am the only male. A mother-and-daughter relationship where both are competing for my affections and both win is also very stimulating. (Although I've never experienced this fantasy, I'd like to.)

•

Two lesbians and myself.

•

Sometimes I think of lovemaking with two women at a time, experiencing moments of passivity and aggression. Generally there is no feeling of love (in the platonic sense) but rather a singular urge for sex and gratification. . . . I've never experienced this fantasy. Although I have some rational feelings as to my performance capabilities, I certainly would not refuse an opportunity to make love to two women at the same time if offered.

5. Power and Achievement (Including Being Considered an Exceptionally Good Lover)

All my daydream sexual fantasies are tied up in being successful in business which is closely related for me to sexual gratification.

•

I fantasize that I am making love to the most exciting, beautiful woman in the world. I drive her wild; she keeps coming back for more, believing I'm the best lover she's ever been with.

•

I fantasize about raping a woman to the point of making her subject to my desires (then stop short of rape).

6. Watching a Woman Perform in a Sexually Enticing Way

When I make love to my wife and am sometimes not really in the most aroused mood, I help things along by fantasizing about a stripteaser I saw in New Orleans several years ago. This girl was fantastic. She skillfully tantalized and titillated everyone in the audience—the women too, I'm sure. She started fully clothed—dancing provocatively to the music; her hips and stomach and even breasts moved seductively. As she took her clothes off and made coy "come get me, sweetheart" moves, I felt my mouth get dry and my dick get hard. It's hard to explain what she did, but her moves were sexier than hell and almost hypnotic. Sort of a Pied Piper—or maybe a better example would be a snake ("penis") charmer. By the time she got down to the G-string (what there was of it) and her bare, beautiful, erect nippled breasts, I was ready to rush on the stage to fuck her. In my fantasy, I do exactly that.

7. Clandestine Sex

A daydream fantasy based on true experience: She was director of a summer employment service in our community and had met with me in my office about our company hiring students for the summer. She was beautiful with blond hair and blue eyes and a sexy, sexy body—though she tried to hide it with business-like clothes. We talked for a while, I agreed to hire two people for two months, then asked if she'd like to, but she had other appointments to keep that afternoon. I asked her about the following day, but she said it was better not to since she was married and in a small town people do talk. Two weeks later, by chance—or fate—we bumped into each other at a local restaurant. I was leaving as she came in alone. I asked if I could join her and she consented. As we drank our beers I knew that she was as interested and as turned on as I. I moved my leg against her as she sat across the table. She responded and we were both so horny we couldn't stand it. "Where can we go?" I asked. She said she didn't know of a safe place and really should leave—while she could. I offered to drive her back to the office and she accepted. Although she sat properly against the passenger's door of my station wagon, we took hands immediately and the vibes and heat were incredible. I reached across to put my hand on her thigh and she moved toward me. We were both so hot, I drove past her office and out into the country. We parked the car in a treed area of some private farm and made fantastic love in the back of the wagon. We still get together every so often and find a hidden place for our affairs.

8. Wife or Lover Having Sexual Relations with Another Man

During sexual relations, I fantasize that my wife is having relations with other men or that she is having sex with a Black man in order to get satisfaction.

•

It is very exciting to think that some big stud is fucking my wife and her legs are spread out and she's screaming and having one big orgasm after another.

•

When we have sex, I get very stimulated if my wife makes up stories about fucking other men and goes into detail about what their penises feel like going in and out and how she is feeling and how they seduce her and how they ravage her.

9. Sex with a Younger Woman

I get turned on by the sexy nymphs who walk down the street with their long hair and firm, lithe bodies. When I see one I fantasize how I'd stop to talk with her, invite her for some dinner, perhaps dancing at a disco, and go to her apartment or rent a motel room to make love all night. I could come again and again in her young tight cunt and teach her the joys of love only a man (in contrast to a boy) can know.

•

I fantasize about seducing the Lolitas of this world and would like to realize this fantasy very much.

10. Sex with a Woman Other than the One Having Intercourse with at the Time

Susan and I have been married for over fifteen years. So sex is more of a "have to" thing than an exciting adventure. I met Jane recently at a convention. We missed most of the convention—staying in her room making love all day, all night. I've never been so turned on, never made love so long and so many times in a row. Didn't know I was capable of it anymore. The memory of Jane gets me extremely horny, and I find I often think of her when making love to Susan. I feel kinda guilty about it. But then I think—I can please Susan better sexually with such arousing thoughts.

Popular as these fantasies are, there are many more....

SPECIAL FANTASIES

Bondage

She is the sexiest woman I've ever seen, with long black hair, flashing white teeth, and the greatest figure imaginable. Her breasts are big and voluptuous. She's a nurse at the clinic where I work and during the day recently I've been fantasizing doing a whole trip with her. I imagine us working late one night when everyone else has gone home. I walk into one of the examination rooms and there she is. I instruct her to take off her clothes and lie on the examination table. When she does this I take some of the rubber tubing and tie her down on the table. I spread her legs and arms and tie them to the metal supports on the sides of the table. She looks so helpless and so ready for whatever I have to offer. I go to her pussy and open the lips and play with them. I take a feather and tickle her clitoris and the lips of her pussy. Then I lick it with my tongue and suck her clitoris and put my tongue up inside her. She squeals with delight, but is still bound so she can't move. I tantalize her in these ways for more than an hour till she's begging me to fuck her. I then take out my hard penis and stand above her and rub it on the outside of her wet pussy. She keeps begging and begging me and I just tease her. Then I insert my penis slightly. She tries to get it farther in but can't because she's tied down. She's going crazy and wants me to fuck her deep so bad; but I won't comply yet. I hold to her huge breasts and suddenly start thrusting my penis deep inside her, and she screams with ecstasy as we both come harder and deeper than ever before.

Photographer

I fantasize that I'm a famous photographer (like in the movie *Blow-Up*). The most exciting model in the world has come to have me photograph her. I have her move and pose in every exciting position available. Her clothing gets skimpier as we go on. Finally, as I'm standing above and she's sensually lying on her side smiling seductively, I put down my camera and take out my hard cock. She pulls me down on top of her and sucks my cock. Soon we've undressed each other and are making mad passionate love. I had thoughtfully put my camera on automatic and continued snapping pictures of us in all our sensuous positions.

Sex with a Woman of a Different Race

I fantasize about having sex with a voluptuous Jamaican woman—dark and beautiful. When I vacationed in Jamaica I saw so many women that excited me, but was afraid to start anything 'cause they might not want to. I dream about a dark woman with large breasts. I meet her at a café. She's dressed in a bright orange dress and high heels, with a white gardenia in her hair. We talk. I invite her to dinner and dancing. She accepts and we go to a "local" night club she knows of with authentic Jamaican music. As we dance I can feel her sexy body against me. Soon I have a hard-on, but she doesn't seem to mind as we continue to move erotically together with the music. Soon I'm intoxicated by her, the rum drink, and the atmosphere. We start sharing long, soul kisses during the slow dances. I caress her breasts with my hand as we dance (secretly so others can't see). I can feel her big breasts and hard nipples. I can also feel her cunt pushing against me. I ask her when we can go and she takes me to her apartment nearby. As I undress her, I can't believe the good smooth feeling of her skin and how sexy she is. As I'm sucking her breasts she plays with my erect penis and begs me to fuck her with it. I penetrate her hot, wet vagina and come almost immediately because of the excitement. But I'm hard again almost instantly and we make love till dawn and exhaustion.

Incest

Once with a woman with whom I could not have an erection, I fantasized about my sister and a girl I know being together on a couch—my sister gently touches the girl all over—and gradually lowers her panties. At this point I had a wonderful erection.

Golden Shower

My lover positions her cunt right above my upper chest. I can see her dark pink lips and the hair around them. I start to masturbate myself and as I reach the point just before I come I moan and she lets go with warm urine all over my chest and neck. I come immediately feeling a hot glow inside and outside my body. This fantasy is used to give me a super, warm orgasm when I masturbate.

Masturbating with a Partner

I actually did this with a former lover and think of it often while masturbating. She and I play with each other for a while and coat our bodies with oil. Then we lie on our backs at a planned position so our legs are touching and we can see the other person's genital area. We each start masturbating ourselves and watching the other. We move in rhythm with each other and it intensifies. As she starts to come she moans, closes her eyes, and I can see and feel her body stiffen. I'm terribly excited by now and as I watch her give herself an orgasm and hear her moan with pleasure, I start to come also. The sperm shoots out on my stomach and her side. She opens her eyes and smiles lovingly.

Sexual Relations With Animals

A large dog comes into my house and starts sniffing all around. I only have on a skimpy robe and he starts sniffing me. When he gets to my penis I notice it starts getting hard from the attention. I put some gravy (from the dinner of the previous evening) on my penis and he sniffs and licks it frantically. What a great feeling. I keep putting the gravy on and he keeps lapping it off. My penis is throbbing and on the verge of orgasm. Finally I can't stand it anymore and use my hand to jack off as the dog is licking me. Sure would like to find the right dog and do this in reality.

Menstruation

I have one basic masturbation fantasy that I have every time I masturbate—and something I actually experience occasionally. I am mounted on the back of the woman I'm married to milking her breasts, plunging deep into her. While she pulls me in, I wiggle from side to side and experience a simultaneous orgasm. We're standing, while I am behind her actively fucking, she's standing there supporting my activity and not passionate herself. She is menstruating and it is dripping down her legs.

Amputation

My one-time fantasy concerns amputation. The only reason I buy *Penthouse* is to read the letters to the editor "from" amputees. I am convinced the letters are faked, probably written by some imaginative member of the magazine staff, but they nevertheless turn me on. My strongest sexual arousal now (outside of actual relations with my wife) is provoked by amputee fantasies. I can't explain the fetish, other than to say I think I was born with it. I'm ashamed of it, because I think it's abnormal. But I can't control it. I fantasize each of the girls in my recollections as having one or no legs, always off above the knee, near the hip. I actually saw a one-legged girl, young, long black hair, on crutches in a restaurant a few months ago, and I was surprised at the intensity of my reaction—feverish, disoriented, loss of appetite. She has since become part of my fantasies. I don't know what I'd do if I ever actually came into physical contact with an amputee. "Blow a fuse," as the *Penthouse* letters say, I suppose. Infrequently, during intercourse, I'll knead my wife's hip and imagine it is a stump. Weird, indeed. But indeviant.

Black Magic and Snakes

I have wild fantasies about having sex with men and women in some of the cult groups who practice black magic.

•

I fantasize fucking a witch.

•

I fantasize about women and snakes (those with lines)—I fantasize about snakes writhing about the woman when she is having an orgasm.

PROFILES

A man's sexual fantasies are very personally his and present explicit profiles of what is important to him in many aspects of life. Some of the fantasies are romantic, some are wistful, and some are quick and to the point. But all tell us something about the fantasizer.

Often people worry about the substance of their fantasies—afraid the fantasies are weird or somehow "wrong." But we all have a wide variety of thoughts, and probably ones we are most concerned about having are really very "normal" and commonly shared. Better to know and understand our fantasies than to try to deny or suppress them. And the derivations of our thoughts are usually quite logical and rational.

We don't have to act on our sexual fantasies—and usually in fact find it practical not to do so. We can, however, enjoy them, communicate them to others, if we choose, and most of all, use them as tools toward self-understanding and acceptance, for through understanding comes growth and an ability to relate more genuinely with others. In that spirit the following men revealed the most intimate parts of themselves—their private thoughts.

DAVID holds a high-level management position in a large northeastern concern. He is 40 years old, lives in the city, is a "semi"-active member of the Presbyterian Church, and is married for the second time. The father of four children, he was born and spent his earlier years in the West Indies where his father was a successful businessman. David has lived on both U.S. coasts as well as in the Midwest. He has an advanced college degree, as does his wife, and has a mixed ethnic background of Caucasian, Black, and Native American. He says that he masturbates on the average of once a week (more when away from home traveling) and thinks about sex several times during the day. His sexual orientation is primarily heterosexual, but he has had some bisexual encounters in groups.

Daydream Fantasies

1. Being in a crowded subway one often gets close to fellow passengers. On a number of occasions they have been quite exciting, for example:
   a. The subway was packed like sardines. An attractive woman had her ass right against my penis with the train shaking back and forth. We kept rubbing against each other. She pressed harder, using the shaking of the train to best advantage. After three stops more people got on and it was even more crowded. Everyone had to readjust to let the additional passengers in. At that time she turned to her left side with her left hand in her raincoat, which placed it directly on my penis. We looked at each other pleasantly while not saying a word. The jostling of the train, her caresses—

one hell of a way to start the day. This happened about six months ago and I have thought of it often. We saw each other once more in the subway about three weeks after it happened but we were so far away from each other. While we were getting off I think she was trying to find me and I certainly was trying to find her. We got lost in the crowd. Perhaps someday . . . It has helped me in masturbating. During some sexual relations I have fantasized her into the situation.

b. Just two weeks ago on the subway a chunky, Spanish woman about 45 carrying a shopping sack was next to me. She held the sack handle with two hands and right next to my dick. She —I—"we" couldn't move because we were literally forced into a corner facing each other. Five stops later she was holding my dick in her hand. I came at the fourth stop. When the train was stopped, and letting people on, she kept rubbing and I came. We separated at the next stop because she had to get off. She invited me off but I had a meeting to attend at 9:00 A.M. Probably wouldn't have gone anyway. Have thought about her and the situation sometimes since.

2. Flying on business trips there are some fine sights to see. For example:

a. About fifteen years ago on Central Airlines flying to Dallas, the two hostesses were really fine. One in particular had one of the most sensuous ways about her. She has been in my daydreams for years, even a masturbation now and then. Unfortunately, we didn't make it, but her co-hostess and I did at about 20,000 feet in the air in the rest room. It was the day I was drafted to go in the Army. It wasn't that good —but a great way to start your army career.

b. Going on many other trips one does observe

and dream and on some occasions (when I try—it usually works out one of three attempts) it can turn into a dinner, dancing, and more often than not spending the rest of the night together.

3. Church & Communiy Affairs—One meets the most interesting people and when in meetings there is ample time to dream.

   a. Church—Adult Education Committee of which I'm chairman. There are two really tough women. My daydreams of them include having both of them at the same time—might someday. . . .

   b. YMCA—Board of which I was a member included a professional who was not interested in me but my wife. He had her a few times. We were almost together twice, but I did daydream of them together a few times.

   c. A volunteer civic group that met in regard to city and county library matters included two females—both of whom really turned me on. I was with each one "almost" but not quite intimately—interestingly enough they both got divorced and one married the other's prior husband.

4. Teaching Situations—Both in seminars and the classroom one can trail off in observing the interesting men and women. While having had closure (being together sexually) only from seminars (*never* in the classroom) the tall, short, skinny, chunky, fair, dark, etc., of those guys and gals can give pleasurable daydream trips.

Masturbatory Fantasies

1. The primary manner I've been successful in masturbating is by talking to someone over the phone. For example:

   a. Being in a hotel room after having gone out to

dinner and retired for the evening. Either called my wife or a friend and in the process of talking fondled myself and gotten into sexual conversations. These conversations could be: about us doing it or how we did it; about the other person and someone else; while the other person is with someone else.

b. The above had happened at work too. One Saturday when no one was in the office but me, I called a very attractive and intelligent woman. We talked really for the first time about sex over the phone. Both of us masturbated successfully. I practically hit the ceiling. Subsequent to that we did get together. It was really great because many barriers were broken. We practically raped each other when we got together.

2. Another way is when being with my wife or a woman friend—we both masturbate together. Talking to each other really helps each one of us get off—then afterwards there is the closeness which is warm and very reassuring. Other than watching Ann-Margret on TV, I've never been able to successfully masturbate without talking to someone—in person or on the phone.

Fantasies During Sexual Relations

1. Doing it while talking about doing it with others and how it was with others.
2. With three or more people together, I fantasize myself into being able to do it "all night"—seven, ten, twelve times in four, five, or six hours and then doing it again.
3. I think of sucking a man when making love to a woman or her sucking a man or a woman—it really turns me on.
4. Intellectually stimulating and challenging people make me want them. Thinking things abstractly or

logically carries me to a level of desire for the "total" person. .

In answer to the question "Do you open or close your eyes during orgasm?" David replied:

At the point of orgasm closed usually, but when interacting before and after my eyes are open in intercourse; when masturbating, they are almost always closed.

David is a successful businessman, active in his community, who also allows his creative energies to flow toward a variety of sexual interests and activities. He and his wife enjoy their sex life and have experimented with an "open" marriage and group sex. Although such experimentation is not uncommon, some couples are devastated by the results while others find their relationship revitalized. David's experience sounds as if it might fit the latter category.

His airline fantasies are typical of many travelers. Obviously the airlines for years have promoted or at least reinforced such imaginary adventures with advertising and the attractiveness of flight attendants. Many of the elements which seem to be important enhancements for sexual encounters in our society are combined to some degree in an airplane trip. It can be a diversion and refuge from the tension and routine of work. The businessman is often alone on these flights. There's even a slight element of bondage to this experience as passengers are relatively helpless and immobile during the flight and at least minimally restrained by seat belts and the limitations of space. Being catered to by friendly flight attendants of the opposite sex can be quite seductive. There is also an element of fantasy and a clandestine aspect to an airborne seduction. For the more daring, actually to have sex with someone in an almost public place would take quite a bit of ingenuity and nerve. The challenge is a turn-on to many adventurous travelers. Being thousands of feet up and above everyday problems can also stimulate a desire for a sexual encounter. It can engender a brief sense of freedom from obligations and a feeling that somehow what happens in this "neutral" area in the sky won't have to be dealt with or carried any further upon landing. Many of the popular stimulants cited by men are combined, to some degree, in this airline seduction.

David also mentions another form of sexual encounter which is becoming more and more popular—telephone sex, an exciting way to fill lonely hours in a strange town, and to communicate with a desired person. Also, it's relatively safe. There's a built-in protection from getting too intimate or involved.

David illustrates the sexual spectrum that many men embrace—from the quick anonymous encounters to an interest in and yearning for the "total" person. He shares the fantasies of most men of having unusual sexual prowess and endurance, and is frank about his occasional fantasies and desires for sex with other men. Such interests are quite common in both sexes, but often difficult for the American man to admit and incorporate into his sexual image.

MIKE is a 19-year-old West Coast student majoring in physics. His ethnic background is Asian-American. He was brought up as a Moslem but is no longer an active member of that religion. He says he masturbates on the average of every other week and thinks about sex about every half hour. He is heterosexual and presently dissatisfied with his sex life because of the recent breakup of a relationship.

Daydream Fantasies

I once saw a cellist who was very attractive playing in concert. A female cellist has to shimmy her ass up to the edge of the chair, keeps her back straight, and holds the cello between her legs. I instantly began fantasizing. I saw her as my girlfriend. We made love one afternoon and we were basking in the postcoital glow. I said, "Hey, will you play me something on your cello?" "What would you like to hear?" "Something you know well and won't mess up if I distract you." "What are you going to do?" "You'll see." She gets up and assumes a cellist's position in the nude. She is barely on the edge of the chair. I uncomfortably place myself under the chair so that I can lick her while she plays. She begins a piece and I begin to lick her clitoris and fondle it with my tongue. She begins to moan but she keeps playing. As I fantasize how I eat her, I can even feel it. Soon she begins to climax and the music disappears. She puts the cello down and I lick her to orgasm. Afterwards, I just rock her in my arms.

Another fantasy (daydream) goes like this. I meet a svelte, dark-haired young woman in a train station. Without words, we are attracted to each other. I whisper to her, "I want to make love to you tonight." I look into her wide brown eyes and she raises her eyebrows and nods. We miss our trains and check into a motel room for a night. We silently undress. I caress her. She begins to caress my neck up to my ear and slips her tongue into my ear. (This always drives me wild.) I caress her now. I kiss her mouth, neck, I dwell on her breasts. I suck on one and massage the other. All the time her hands are all over my body, rubbing and squeezing. I leave her breasts and go directly to her cunt. I lick for a little while. She disengages and puts my cock in her mouth, while fondling my balls. I disengage and we screw. Me on top for about the first half. Then we reverse and she gets on top. She gyrates her hips and does some of the most wonderful things I can imagine. I wonder where she learned that. She climaxes and then I climax. She collapses on top of me with a smile on her face. I say, "When did you learn that?" She replies, "I am a ballerina." I say, "Oh. Well, I'm a theoretical physicist, we'd make a perfect couple." She says, "I'm sorry, I'm married." Not another word is spoken. We fall asleep in that position. I know that when I wake up in the morning, she won't be there. I'll never see her again, and that's partially why it's so good with her.

I have these fantasies about once every two or three weeks. They are much more exciting than any pornographic literature. You see, I believe one fucks with one's head, and not one's pelvis. During the rest of the month I just go over sex I've had with women I know. I really have these fantasies, and they will probably stick around for a few more months. I have never lived through these fantasies. The others I have are just replays of previous experiences. Given the opportunity, I would gladly live this out. I'll probably act these out, one of these days, with someone.

I usually have daydreams about someone I love, since I would rather "make love" than "have sex." Do you know what I mean? I do not masturbate with the above two fantasies.

Masturbatory Fantasies

To really excite me, I need fantasies which are very real, so I replay past experiences.

I recently lost a girlfriend, and I fantasize about her. Here is one fantasy with a slight twist, something *not* a replay.

She and I are in the living room of my apartment. I say, "Let's make love." We go into the bedroom. We undress while smiling. (I learned not to try to undress a girl.) We start. We have oral sex. Then we fuck. First me on top. We change positions a few times. She comes a few times. I end up under her. We are approaching a simultaneous orgasm! As we come, I spank her. She moans and pants. When it's over, I hold her in my arms and talk a while.

I have not had this thought very often. I usually replay old times. I do not spank her in my daydreams. I used this fantasy once. I have never harmed her in real life. Once I asked if she wanted me to, and she said no.

I don't want to spank her really. It's just that sometimes when I was angry with her, I'd just keep it down. I'd fantasize about spanking her, and that would get it out of my system. If she wanted me to, I probably would have. I would do anything if she wanted me to. But when I'm not angry with her, I'd have no compulsion to strike her. I'm the tender kind of lover.

Fantasies During Sexual Relations

I have not had sexual relations so often as to need a fantasy to spice it up. I am so interested in lovers, and I concentrate so well, that the real thing is much better than a fantasy.

I lost my girlfriend. If I ever started to make it with someone, and started pretending that my partner was my ex-girlfriend, I would just stop. I have refused to screw women who have propositioned me because I know I would fantasize about my ex-girlfriend. It's the cheapest deception I know of. That's part of the price of love.

If I screw someone or make love to someone, I want my whole soul and all my love to be with me. Isn't that what making love is all about—the union of skin and souls?

Having a sexual fantasy during sex is like bringing a ham sandwich to a feast.

Mike's fantasies exemplify the romantic and sensitive nature of a number of men's erotic thoughts.

His fantasy about the ballerina centers around the excitement of a quick and intense encounter with the romantic and semitragic possibility of not meeting again. The clandestine and existential nature of the affair often adds intensity.

Mike also has a desire to personalize the women in his fantasies and envision them holistically instead of as faceless bodies. He appears to be a creative and sensitive person who wants sex to be an important and integrated part of his life. In this he represents a growing number of men who are challenging the traditional "locker room" approach to sex and who are making it a much richer and intimate part of their lives.

He is reacting to being hurt by a loved one. His explanation of how he shows his anger by refusing to have an erection, then expressing that anger through a spanking fantasy, is insightful and can be extremely helpful in dealing with a relationship and understanding the complexities and psychological entwining of one's own sexuality.

His philosophy with respect to sex is well capsulized in some of his clever one-liners.

"I believe one fucks with one's head and not one's pelvis."
"I would rather make love than have sex."
"Isn't that what making love is all about—the union of skin and souls?"
and "Having a sexual fantasy during sex is like bringing a ham sandwich to a feast."

WILLIS is a Black 30-year-old police officer on the East Coast. Raised by working-class parents in the rural South, he was, but is no longer, a member of the Holiness Church. He is divorced and has one child.

He says he masturbates several times a week and thinks of sex several times daily. He finds sexually arousing "any book that shows female genitals" and the movies *Deep Throat, The Devil in Miss Jones,* and *Behind the Green Door.* Literature and films have affected his fantasies by "opening the door to unlimited ways of giving and receiving pleasure."

Willis is heterosexual and content with his sex life.

Daydream Fantasies

When daydreaming, I simply think back on past sexual experiences with particularly responsive or vocal women. And if these daydreams are about women that were exceptionally good in one way or the other, fellatio, anal, oral-anal, spanking, etc., I must masturbate immediately.

I often fantasize about women that I have on the "line" (waiting list) but haven't made love to yet, about how good, responsive, or freaky they will be. Now mind you, I don't go in for the way-out freaks, for instance I won't let a woman spank me or stick anything other than her tongue up my ass.

Masturbatory Fantasies

While masturbating my fantasies almost always change to nice situations I've been involved in. Such as having one woman masturbate me while another one gives me a blow job, or fucking one while the other one is playing with the clitoris of the one I'm fucking (in the front seat of a station wagon, in a moderately crowded parking lot yet!).

Sometimes I'll think about certain women that I've been with who were totally uninhibited, such as one (a lesbian) that enjoys reaming my asshole with her tongue and masturbating me to get me really excited and then fucking before I get my nut.

I have so many fantasies that it's hard to find the right one to describe. For instance, there is this one woman (25 years old) that likes for me to finger fuck her with three fingers while kissing her breasts and then she will lick her own pussy juices from my fingers before we fuck, and she really gets turned on.

One of my fantasies that I always have but haven't quite had the opportunity to experience yet is being in bed with two women where I'm eating one out while she is eating the second one out who is giving me a blow job and we all explode at the same time.

I would like to add that while my fantasies might seem weird, no one has ever been hurt or disappointed, and women always leave my bed wanting to come back. The important thing is never to force anyone to do anything against their will. Do only what they want to do and then only if they enjoy it. For instance, I have performed a 69 for more than an hour before fucking. While it turns her on, and she gets many nuts, I haven't dropped a load in a woman's mouth in more than five years even though many have tried unsuccessfully to make me come in their mouths.

Fantasies During Sexual Relations

While making love, I think about anything but sex! I think about rain, war, cars, anything but sex. In this way I can delay my own orgasm almost indefinitely, and I have yet to make love to a woman (in my adult life) who wasn't totally satisfied.

When she is "fucked out" and can't take any more, then I think about sex and how good she is and force my own nut and reduce both of our bodies to sawdust.

Willis appears to be comfortable with his sexuality and enjoys exploring new possibilities—without forcing the issue.

His nonsexual thoughts during sexual relations are quite common to men. Many use fantasy to control and delay their orgasms. One man goes over the 1947 batting line-up of the Brooklyn Dodgers, another thinks about what he should do to promote his business, another says he concentrates on his plans for the next day. Women, on the other hand, don't usually feel they have to delay their orgasms, so fantasy is rarely used by them in this way. However, women not enjoying a sexual situation may find themselves using nonsexual thoughts to distract themselves. This was particularly true in the past for traditional married women who "endured" the obligatory sex with their husbands.

Useful as nonsexual fantasies are for prolonging sexual activity, it is true that men have their most intense and enjoyable orgasms when they "let themselves go" in their lovemaking and allow themselves personal surrender to their partner and the moment.

Prolonging sex, especially if a man has the tendency to orgasm quickly after penetration, may be important and appreciated by a woman when it gives her time to orgasm as well. However, most women are especially aroused and fulfilled when their partners relinquish control and share in emotional and sexual surrender.

Everyone must find their own comfortable equilibrium between control and "letting go." In finding this equilibrium a man should remember that, if the sex is good, there is usually time for more leisurely intercourse following his first orgasm.

DON is a WASP 53-year-old physician who does sex therapy on the West Coast. Originally from the Midwest, he was raised as a Baptist. Previously divorced and father of four children, he presently lives with a woman. He masturbates monthly, thinks about sex several times daily, is heterosexual in his sexual activity and satisfied. Don finds books about the erotic art of Japan arousing as well as the movie *The Hustler*. (Like many men in the study, he considers Ann-Margret very attractive and sexy.) He says, however, that literature and movies have not really affected his sexual fantasies.

Daydream Fantasies

An affair with a movie star (i.e., Diana Rigg). Also think about lifting up the skirt of an attractive woman and running my hand up her leg.

Masturbatory Fantasies

Practically none. Occasional thought of partner. Most masturbation is with a female partner.

Fantasies During Sexual Relations

Practically none that I can recall. Fantasy of having intercourse right away. Usually stay with what I'm doing.

I fantasize very little about sex and can usually fulfill these fantasies of a desire. For instance, when I am meeting a new partner, I fantasize how she will be and how I will be. Playful, shy, avoiding, or welcoming. I avoid fantasizing rejection. Oh yes, also fantasize having a large penis, even though I regard myself as quite adequate. Knowing better, I fantasize an evening or entire day of continuous sexual contact.

Don probably has more fantasies than he mentioned, but is typical of many physicians and lawyers who are either reluctant to articulate their feelings or lack variety and elaboration in their fantasies. Very likely he is feeling time pressures. Also, both types of professionals are trained to be terse, quick, decisive. The questionnaire responses of these professionals were often very similar to those of blue-collar workers with decidedly less education.

Don seems to be comfortable and open with regard to his sexuality. He is also aware of the sexual fears and concerns that he and most men have, such as rejection, penis size, and the desire to perform with almost unlimited capacity.

ROBERT is a 22-year-old college graduate leaving for a two-year stint overseas with the Peace Corps. He is single, from a white middle-class background, is still active in the Presbyterian Church, and has lived in both urban and rural areas in the Northeast. He almost never masturbates, is not satisfied with his sex life, and occasionally has sexual fantasies.

Daydream Fantasies

I think of sexual promiscuity with various girls I have met during the day.

The frequency of the occurrence varies in direct proportion with the bodily features and attractiveness of the particular girl I met. You, yourself, have provided me with very nice, shall I say, "food for fantasy."

I also have this fantasy sometimes when I masturbate. It perhaps began in my latter years.

I have only had sex with one girl and she was terribly ugly—the experience is one I don't like to remember. I don't fantasize about that experience and never did. We had what is commonly called a "gang-bang."

Yes, I'd like to act out this thought. I can think of few men who wouldn't like to be promiscuously active. However, I can think of few or none of the people I know who are. Most are just talkers.

Masturbatory Fantasies

I rarely masturbate and have little desire to. I would rather find another outlet for sexual expression and satisfaction. In many ways I am very naive about the world; however, I like it better that way. I like so-called naive girls better because I feel sophistication can destroy a person. The most beautiful people are unsophisticated, innocent, and sincere.

Fantasies During Sexual Relations

The only time I did have sexual intercourse, I had no fantasies. The only thing I remember was a nauseating sensation. Don't get me wrong, I still believe in the euphoric, gratifying feeling two people can gain from a sexual experience. However, I have yet to experience it. The only girl I really loved, I made the mistake of idealizing to the point where she was untouchable to me. I loved her on a different, more philosophical plane, showering her with poems, candy, and flowers. Somehow the realism, personal rapport, and mutual dependence needed for an effective relationship never developed. I never had sex with her because I was more concerned with building a relationship encompassed by my idealized concept of love. Now I fantasize being a cruel, uncaring individual, having sex with her and performing different erotic sex acts. Perhaps because I want to get some kind of revenge to satisfy my mind. When I was idealistic I became only a friend, if I were to be a brutish heathen, I would have been her lover. I have always viewed sex as an artistic means of expression, it can be a very beautiful thing or a very empty thing. At this point in my life I have been fulfilled mentally because I have felt love, but feel empty at the same time. I wish I had time to organize my thoughts more; however, I hope what I have said has been of some help in your work.

Robert expresses so well the dilemma in which a number of men find themselves at some time in life, and which should lead women to consider the very strong role which they may play in encouraging the double standard and impersonal sex from men. Hopefully, experience will help Robert settle somewhere between his idealizing of a "love" relationship and his fantasies of cruelty and revenge.

BILL is a 19-year-old from a large midwestern city and works as a chauffeur. He's from a white working-class environment, did not finish high school, and is divorced. He says that he masturbates about once a month and thinks about sex several times daily. He finds the pictures in sexually explicit magazines arousing and was turned on by the movie *The Happy Hooker*. His orientation is heterosexual.

Daydream Fantasies

My only fantasy is to have sex with an older woman —between 30–35. I don't have it very often. My fantasy has not come true yet, but I'll keep working on it and I'm sure it will.

Masturbatory Fantasies

I masturbate now and then, but only if there is no woman around to have sex with. I do get horny quite often, but I usually find a woman. I really don't have any masturbating fantasies.

Fantasies During Sexual Relations

No fantasies during sexual relations. I think about the woman I am making love to and how to please her to the best of my ability.

Although Bill doesn't report a great variety of fantasies, his concern about pleasing the woman to whom he's making love contrasts with the sexual attitudes of young men of his socioeconomic and educational group twenty or more years ago. The effects of Masters and Johnson's studies as well as the increased sexual openness and concern with women's sexual needs often espoused by popular magazines such as *Playboy* and *Penthouse* have affected men in all walks of life. Most men now see their criteria as great lovers to center around the fulfillment of their partner. These efforts are positive in their concern for the "other." We can hope that this concern is sincere in itself and not just another means to personal achievement—score keeping by a scorer. A woman can sense the difference and responds accordingly.

GEORGE is a 63-year-old widower who lives in the Southwest where he is a real estate developer. Since the death of his wife, he says his sex life has not been satisfactory—saying his wife is a hard act to follow. He is, however, still enthusiastic, with no plans to retire "before 95."

Daydream Fantasies

For the most part any thoughts I have in this line are of and about my dead wife. We had over a period of twenty-one years what was and still is in my memory a beautiful and quite fantastic relationship. I enjoy remembering her, and yet at the same time the memory can be and is quite painful because I miss her so very much. If I am daydreaming about her and it is a physical situation where I cannot jack off, my thoughts still begin and quickly turn to sexual matters. One of the best things for me in remembering her is that there are so few memories of her that are not sexual. She dressed to please me in any or all situations that allowed it. I remember my youngest son counting forty-seven pairs of shoes one evening. All but two pairs—her hiking boots and a pair of sandals for the beach—had heels five inches or better. She always thought her knees were too heavy; I loved them just the way they were, and still do. She worked for the last eight years or so, and unless I was away for some reason there was never a morning that I did not give her a bath and dress her. She understood that I preferred garters, and she almost always wore them. I doubt that she owned more than six pairs of pantyhose in her life not counting the special open-crotch ones we bought for her. I like to think that I can remember exactly how she smelled, her hair, her armpits, her belly and pussy and hands and knees and feet, her butt and her asshole, all of her and each place a separate and different, wonderful odor. I recall her moods. She was as deadly and as dangerous as a hungry hunting falcon when protecting her children, and as gentle as a brood hen when caring for them. She was a women's libber all of her life and not one of the thousands of men she fucked over ever knew she was one. She was a two-bit Tijuana whore or the one asked to pour at a hat-and-gloves-on tea. She was a strong and moving force in local politics, a forceful and articulate speaker. She was a quiet and understanding listener. She kept important or harmful secrets like an Indian brave and loved to gossip like a magpie. She was an impatient and inept hunter but a skilled and expert fisher-woman. She had for me, and raised for herself, two tall, straight, honest, happy boys. They were C students that can swim like fish, shoot expert with every weapon made, love and play music with any instrument in the band, and fight like wet bobcats. On a long hike they always carry the packs of the little ones and often carry the little ones too. She taught them to laugh often but that it was all right to cry only when it was someone else who hurt. She could weep at the death of a goldfish but I'm positive would and could have killed swiftly and without mercy or remorse with proper provocation.

She loved and lived her life with every breath she took. She had an insatiable curiosity, absorbed, retained, and played back information on anything from a book to how to build a proper compost pile. But most and best of all she was SEX; she could and would argue down any reason against it, and her body and being were history's best argument for it. I knew her body better than anyone in the world except her. She knew every sensation it could offer her and searched for and willingly accepted them anytime, anyplace, anywhere. She climaxed from a soft kiss in the hollow of her neck or a sound, cracking whack across the cheeks of her ass. She could fuck the juice and strength from six young men and curse and deride them as quitters, or come and fall asleep while sucking my big toe. She suffered through a session of bondage with the lithe grace of a gypsy girl or when dominant showed all the loving kindness of a marauding Hun. She flaunted my slave brand to the world but would have pissed Lincoln's beard full if ever she had him under her high heels.

It's hard for me to judge whether or not you will feel that what I have said here falls into your definition of fantasies. What I have written is what I daydream about, and that seems to be what you asked me for. These thoughts would almost never overlap while in the act of sex. They often overlap while I'm jacking off.

Fantasies During Sexual Relations

I find that I fantasize very little when I am having sex. There are times and have been times when the person that I was with was so inhibited that they performed in what was to me a boring or uninteresting way. Often when in this situation I find that the only way that I can keep myself interested enough to do them any good at all is to allow myself to think about how nice it would be to be able to give them the kinds and types of sex that I know are good for both of us. I have also found that there are times when women of this type like to hear me talk of doing other things to them, and although turned on by what they are hearing they still will not allow for it to happen.

There are many ways of relating. The ways are not as important as the respect and fulfillment two people find with each other. Besides substitution or planning for the future, fantasy also includes replays of the past. In his fantasy and remembrances of his former wife, George paints an idyll of enjoyment and love which would be difficult for any couple—whatever their ways of relating—to surpass.

Stan, in the following, insightfully describes the source of his enema fantasy. He also wisely allows himself to enjoy this sexual fantasy instead of guiltily suppressing it, in which case it might pop up in a masked form. He realizes the natural association between this fantasy and past realities and is fortunate to have a wife who understands his special form of arousal. As with George, Stan loves and is able to communicate with his wife. Acceptance is important in any relationship, the individual's acceptance of himself and the specialness of his partner as well.

STAN is a 55-year-old successful businessman living on the East Coast.

Daydream Fantasies

I have an enema fantasy—based on an experience in my youth. . . . It occurred when I was in the hospital following an appendix operation. . . . A firm nurse marches in with a tray covered with a towel . . . under the towel is an assortment of enema gadgets. . . . To my shocked gaze she pulls back the bed covers and exposes me as I lie on my back. . . . In a businesslike manner she gets busy. . . . Before I fully comprehend what is happening . . . I am benumbed. . . . She is greasing up my asshole with Vaseline . . . then

71

quickly and smoothly sliding in a long black rubber tube. . . . The other end of the black tube flops up loosely. . . . She snips away at it with scissors . . . presumably to get the right length for the operation. . . . Satisfied, she attaches the free end of the tube to a large, white canister . . . filled with liquid. . . . I understand it to contain a soap solution.

She holds the canister aloft . . . siphoning the warm water into my rectum. . . . I am in a state of semishock . . . but also find the sensation pleasurable . . . begin to have an erection. . . . Soon I feel full up. . . . Tell her (I am sobbing now . . . the indignity of it all) that Skane had enough. . . . Firmly she explains that it is *not* quite finished yet . . . I must take it all. . . . I imagine my belly must be swollen, distended. Having given me my fill . . . she is satisfied . . . detaches the white canister . . . and smoothly, comfortably, extracts a long black glistening (with lubricant) tube or nozzle from inside my anus. . . . I watch passingly, horrified, fascinated. . . . I still have a vivid pictorial memory of the black glistening tube emerging from inside and between my thighs . . . and I know I had a stiff thick erection . . . so much so . . . that as I lay . . . still partly benumbed . . . on a bedpan . . . gushing matter in sheer torrents out of my backside . . . I did not push down my erect penis . . . and pissed all over the bed . . . which occasioned much chuck-chucking from the nurse . . . she had to change the sheets . . . and asked me if I was a baby for wetting the bed.

Another of my unrealized (in a sense) or partly realized fantasies . . . I am a well proportioned, strong physically, young man . . . standing stark naked . . . and fucking a woman with magnificent thighs . . . she becomes my wife . . . who has such glorious thighs . . . she lies on the bed . . . her legs up . . . and I in deep . . . my firm buttocks give force to my deep penetration. . . . My wife lifts her bent limbs freely and ecstatically in the air . . . I am standing on the floor . . . fucking with abandon . . . deeply . . . giving and getting supreme pleasure . . . exquisite. . . .

There is this girl at my office . . . she is not beautiful . . . but I find her attractive, sexy. . . . She has an almost plain face . . . but it is a very sweet and open and clear face, clear brown eyes . . . also rather shy . . . she is young. . . .

She is tall . . . has a lovely almost boyish figure . . . but still distinctly feminine. . . . Nicely built, firm . . . she usually comes to work in pants and a light blouse . . . neat, tidy . . . she often stands at her job. . . . I would like to go into her room, quickly . . . warmly . . . loosen her pants . . . also take down her nylon panties . . . comfortably, securely . . . so as not to frighten her . . . she doesn't move . . . stands there . . . and despite herself . . . to her own surprise . . . yielding to my gentle warmth . . . I kneel down behind her . . . open up her buttocks . . . and delicately lick her dear brown asshole.

There is a bad snowfall . . . she can't get home (she lives with her mother) . . . nor can I. . . . Somehow I get her to share a room with me at a nearby luxury hotel . . . do her a favor, actually. . . . I am very fatherly toward her . . . she has a shower . . . wearing a light top only . . . clean and beautiful . . . she steps into the bedroom . . . walks across the carpeted floor . . . gets into bed . . . I only want to keep her warm . . . her adorable light pubic hair . . . to lick her . . . and then gently to fuck between her long, strong thighs. . . . Perhaps I will have her lie relaxed, stretched out on her stomach . . . and penetrate her vagina from behind . . . admiring her sweet, firm, boy-like buttocks. . . .

Masturbatory Fantasies

As a young man, before I was married, I used sometimes to give myself an enema and then masturbate. I also used to fantasize that I was an oriental sultan with a harem of nubile maidens dressed in transparent clothing who disported themselves about a blue-tiled swimming pool. I would watch them quietly, paternally, from a balcony above . . . and summon one whenever necessary for a "quickie."

Some years ago I was undergoing great tension at my work . . . my nerves were getting bad . . . I phoned my wife about it. She told me to come home for lunch. . . . Back at home . . . knowing my enema fascination . . . she had me drop my pants . . . and inserted a hot-water-bottle tube enema (white) into my ass while I lay on my front . . . she gave me a most relaxing warm-water enema. . . . Later, after I had ejaculated and washed myself clean . . . she lubricated my then enormous penis . . . and massaged it beautifully with her finger pressing my asshole. . . . I still remember this vividly . . . it was magnificent . . . and I felt so much better. . . . I still fantasize about this great releasing pleasure.

My wife does not like to "jack me off" . . . she prefers me to wait until she is again available for sexual action.

Fantasies During Sexual Relations

If my fuck is going well . . . I do not fantasize . . . I love to watch my wife . . . her face takes on a dream-like look . . . a smile plays on her lips.

In foreplay I love her powerful thighs . . . I love to lick her asshole . . . then her clitoris . . . (I keep her pubic hair shaved . . . to see her mound of Venus) . . . while I lick her clitoris . . . I gently insert my index finger into her anus . . . and massage her inside . . . stroking her inner thighs with my other hand . . . until with low moans . . . she comes. . . . Then I penetrate and fuck her.

I am now in the 50s and so do not "shoot" so quickly. If I am tired . . . and not sufficiently excited . . . I like my wife to tell me she will pull down my pants tomorrow and give me a powerful enema of strong soap suds. . . . I also picture myself, full up with water, a black tube still sticking out between my white buttocks, and my wife beats me with a belt . . . to give me red stripes. . . . Once I have attained orgasm of course . . . I no longer expect this to happen. In fact I want her to tell me this (if I am slow in "coming") but knowing full well she won't and not really wanting the real thing . . . only the fantasy. Unfortunately my wife gets annoyed about this . . . so it is only occasionally used. . . .

I love to watch my wife . . . feed on her sensuous beauty when I fuck . . . and explode. . . . I prefer her in daylight.

Occasionally, while I am lying on top of my wife and fucking her . . . I like to remind her of the time she was taken to the hospital to have her baby. . . . While she was in the preparation room being shaved (that gave me an exciting idea . . .) by a brusque, unsympathetic Black woman, I had to wait outside. . . . Then I got excited when I saw a nurse come across carrying and shaking happily (she hummed happily) a large, brown, glass-stoppered bottle containing soapy bubbly matter. . . . Instantly I sense what it is for. . . . The nurse disappears. . . . Soon I hear my wife's loud complaints and protests . . . all in pain . . . she is getting an enema, after her shave, and not enjoying it either . . . to judge from her moans. . . .

How I would have longed to shave her and give her an enema then. . . . She now tells me that, come to think of it, it would indeed have been nice and sexy if I could have given these to her myself. The thought of it thrills me. I could almost give her another baby just to carry it out . . . exquisite. . . . She said the shave was awful . . . she was nicked and scratched. The enema was worse . . . just an awful

shove up the ass . . . pumped like hell . . . strong
soap water . . . she felt awful . . . no delicacy at
all . . . shame.

NEIL is a 23-year-old graduate student in international
relations. He says he thinks about sex about every five
minutes and masturbates almost every day as well as
having a fulfilling sexual and emotional relationship
with the woman with whom he's living.

Daydream Fantasies

A strong "daydream" sexual fantasy of mine is to
have a woman friend whom I greatly desire enter my
room uncalled and have sex with me. This once happened to my great embarrassment several years ago.
The woman friend in question was very drunk and I
very asleep. I jumped out of bed and insisted she return to her room. Yet in a similar incident some time
later I did not discourage the woman involved. The
frequency of this fantasy has dropped off over the
years from perhaps once a week to once a month.
This fantasy often overlaps into masturbation fantasies. With the exception of erotic books and magazines and then only in no one's presence, I rarely
fantasize about women I do not personally know. I
find most arousing and satisfying sexual fantasies
where I construct situations with a woman whose
body and personality I am familiar with rather than
some unknown woman whose body and personality
are "sexy." Of these women whom I am familiar with,
I fantasize most often with those who have displayed
some possible sexual interest. My "daydream" sexual
fantasies are usually in response to some stimuli,
sound, smell, or sight that I find arousing in itself or
in reference to some past pleasant experience. Also,
I daydream in response to boredom, but these con-
jured sexual fantasies are definitely second-rate.

Masturbatory Fantasies

My masturbatory fantasies are largely a carry-over, on a more selective basis, of my daydream sexual fantasies. I fantasize a great deal lately during masturbation about A., a woman friend. We are in a quiet, half-lit place; there are no bright colors, mostly whites and browns. I imagine undressing her, giving her a body massage, and then slowly arousing her till she asks me to enter her. I have this fantasy perhaps once a day. I experience this fantasy as a daydream, a masturbatory sexual fantasy (most frequent), and as a sexual fantasy during sexual relations (least frequent). The intensity of this fantasy heightened by the admission on her part that she is still a virgin at 23 and that she has sexual fantasies during sleep or oral sex. (She is, like myself, of Irish-Catholic descent.) I have never experienced this fantasy though I never pass up the chance to touch A. . . . I would like to experience this fantasy, but I am currently with another woman and this would threaten our relationship.

Fantasies During Sexual Relations

The most common sexual fantasy during sexual relations is that I imagine that I am having sex with an unknown woman, a "slut" type of woman, in some bushes at dark. I have this fantasy about once out of every six or seven times I have sex, to "spice up" otherwise ordinary sex.

Like many of the college-educated men in his age group, Neil's sexual fantasies are about women he knows.

He also admits to frequent fantasies and daily masturbation although he is enjoying a fulfilling relationship with a woman. Fantasy therefore is much more than a substitute for an unfulfilling reality because Neil says his reality is great. Fantasizing can be a creative process enhancing a person's sex life. Like Neil, many men masturbate frequently even while enjoying sex regularly with their partners. Sexual fantasies and masturbation can therefore be viewed as special activities along the sexual spectrum—having their own unique value rather than merely being second-class substitues for intercourse.

BROOKS is a writer, in his own words "a WASP writer from D.C., 27. Father is into management, Mom's a housewife. I'm married. I masturbate once or twice weekly, usually by myself. I get turned on by most of the slick porno now out, 'respected' stuff like *Penthouse,* etc. Use it to masturbate in lieu of fantasies sometimes. But, although it's fun stuff—and not too heavy—it's very limiting to creativity. Often, my own fantasies are based on stuff I've seen or read in the media . . . it's shaped my mind in many cases. That can be good, for new ideas, just like you would try a new cookbook recipe occasionally. But on the other hand, sex and cheeseburgers aren't all that similar."

Daydream Fantasies

During the day, I think about sex constantly when I'm around Connecticut and K or M streets, or wherever there are large concentrations of women, which in D.C. seems to be everywhere. But it's not a heavy thing because who wants to pop off during a daydream at the office? I guess my major daydream fantasy is staring down at the women passing my window—particularly those with dresses—flimsy black ones are the best—and wondering how I'd enjoy meeting them in some social situation. Generally, they approach me (in my fantasy) and we trundle off to my place or hers, but that's where the fantasy stops. Except sometimes I wonder what particular women—those with professional airs especial-ly—would look like sans work clothes and in bed.

Masturbatory Fantasies

Like I said, I let the light porno handle my fantasies for me, in many cases. But other ones that I've en-joyed:

An older woman, matronly, well dressed, and serious . . . her seducing me and then, when we're both extremely turned on, her becoming my sexual equal (which means giddy, insecure, and carefree—sorta like me).

I sometimes get off on ejaculations of all kinds—watching *other* guys' sperm dripping or gushing into a woman's mouth or onto her body—both clothed and naked. A couple of times, a guy's sperm on my face.

A well-dressed young woman . . . who, through sexual frolics, both voluntary and forced onto her, becomes very disheveled.

Sometimes . . . making it with a guy. But only sometimes . . . my emotional stability probably would preclude this ever becoming a reality.

My wife doing it with someone else . . . also some-thing my shaky emotions wouldn't be able to handle.

Young girls. Innocents.

Sexy underwear.

Group sex . . .

Fantasies During Sexual Relations

Many of the above, plus a recurring favorite: role switching. I occasionally like to have my wife become the male, seducing me . . . (I even imagined myself dressed as a woman once) and, during coitus, me actually being on bottom, wrapping my legs around her, her on top squeezing my prick with the lips of her cunt, and suddenly, I am taking her cock, she is driving deeper. Wow.

The second party in all of my fantasies, both masturbatory and during relations, generally is someone that I've recently seen. Sometimes someone I know, but never very well dressed, who works in another office in my building, whom my imagination constantly fondles.

I think the main point in all of this is that my fantasies, both masturbatory and during relations, change constantly. Even a fantasy, if one thinks about it often enough, is a reality in itself, and, as such, becomes almost old hat after a while. They've got to change.

Like a number of men in his age group, Brooks is willing to explore the possibilities of what it would feel like to be a woman during sex. The allowance of this fantasy shows a special comfort with his own sexuality. Many men would feel threatened to have such a fantasy because of fears of homosexuality and fears about not being manly. Actually it is quite natural to wonder what the person of the oppposite sex experiences and feels like. This is a common curiosity. Women have fantasies often about what it feels like to be a man during sexual relations, and this fantasy is more than the "penis envy" psychoanalysts have falsely attributed to women. Such fantasies can be useful in bridging male-female sexual gaps, and can help us empathize and improve communication with our partners.

4

Free, White, and Forty

Men in their 40s represent the traditional American male; they are the leaders and movers in this country. Although they are the prototypes, they are also evaluating their lives and reacting to change as their principal stronghold is being chipped away by cultural changes and sexual revolution.

They bought the American Dream. They went to college, joined the "right" fraternity, groomed themselves for the "right" job, married when the "right girl" came along, and settled in suburbia with two cars, 2.5 children, and a summer home on the lake.

They worked hard, believing in the rightness of it all, and waited for the due rewards which would reinforce their efforts and make them happy. They proudly parlayed the liquid assets into tangible signs of their successes—a swimming pool, private schools for the children, the right suburban district, trips to Europe for mom and dad, club memberships, etc. Sometimes it only took a few years, sometimes more. Whatever the cycle was, this American dreamer woke up one day, looked around him, and knew something was missing, something important. Often he grasped for a solution by looking critically at his job. Should he move up faster? Should he move laterally? Should he just chuck the whole thing? But how, given the mortgage, the kids, and his vicariously ambitious wife pushing him—sweetly but firmly—on to bigger and better demonstrations of their worth? What would his parents say if he balked? And how could he, as a corporate failure, look his neighbor in the face again, or explain to his progeny? Chucking it in would be too drastic and scary, and for what guaranteed alternative reward?

Perhaps if I work harder, he rationalizes, I'll be too tired and successful to feel the aching. Perhaps I just have to fill the emptiness with success and it'll be all right. So the momentum increases, the successes increase, and life is so frantic that exhaustion takes the edge off the gaping discomfort. Or if that's not enough, alcohol will numb the senses or at least envelop them with a gossamer finish.

But what about that cute secretary in the office who smiles so seductively?

I must be getting to be a dirty old man, but I have started noticing the attractive girls around the office much more lately. The new secretary hired for our legal typing is looking especially good. I imagine meeting her in a secluded part of the office, running my hand up her thigh, and seducing her.

•

An agency like ours has so many good-looking girls around. I have trouble keeping my mind on my work some days. Some of the girls had lunch with some of the men in the office. After a few drinks, I had trouble keeping my hands to myself. I think often about what it would be like to have sex with a redhead

who works in my department. Bet she's a wild one
in bed.

•

My new secretary has breasts you can't believe. I
don't know how I missed them when I interviewed
her; maybe she had them camouflaged. It's kind of
thrilling to look at her and fantasize, can also be
very distracting. Guess we'll just have to "work late"
some night soon. This is driving me crazy.

I fantasize about that: She's typing a report. It's
six o'clock that evening. Everyone else has left the
office. I ask her to stop at my desk. As she bends
over to look at the paper I'm showing her, I gently
rub her protruding breasts. Her nipples get hard immediately. She starts to pull away but is obviously
enjoying this too. I slowly unbutton her blouse—still
rubbing gently and massaging her erect nipples. Then
I reach up her skirt between her thighs to play with
her. She moves against me and we both stand up,
press our bodies together and feel all rubbery. I
maneuver her to the nearby couch, expose her lus-
cious breasts, and suck them hungrily. She moans,
and soon we've undressed even more and my throbbing penis penetrates her wet cunt and we both go
wild.

•

At an intensive conference, there's nothing better
than a quick lunch and meeting an attractive participant upstairs and making love till the next session
starts. We might even be a bit late.

What about the noon quickies, the massage parlors,
the topless bars the guys enjoy so much?

A great idea, massage parlors. Get relaxed and released in a most enjoyable way.

•

I've been going to a massage parlor down the street
for almost four years now. They know me well and

know I tip heavily, so I can get about whatever I want for my hour. After a hearty massage, I like the girl to go down on me and suck me to the point of coming. Then I put my hand on her crotch and undo her shorts or short skirt (she's already topless). She's usually as aroused as I am and hops on top and moves frantically till we both come. Sometimes, I get on top of her instead. Whatever. It's quick and enjoyable.

•

To spice up a boring, bureaucratic meeting, I look around and fantasize some of the women in the meeting. One woman always acts businesslike. But I bet if she cast her glasses aside, shortened her skirt, and literally let her hair down, she's be fun to be with. One woman talks a lot, and I fantasize getting her in bed and screwing her till she's speechless.

•

There's an exclusive restaurant down the street that has back rooms where a man can have sex with his choice of the waitresses. Besides being enjoyable after a light meal and a couple of drinks, the whole thing can be written off to business—since it's included in the restaurant bill and can be paid for with a major credit card. Dessert anyone?

•

I enjoy meeting my secretary at her nearby apartment on our lunch hour, about twice a week, or whenever the urge is the greatest and the work load the lightest.

•

When I travel to a big city, I generally go to massage parlors for a "thorough" massage.

•

When traveling, I like to check out the parlors. Besides being a great way to deal with tense and tired muscles, it's a great turn-on. Most of the girls are real young nymphs but know how to please a man. Sometimes I worry a little about being recognized in one of these places, but that also adds a little excitement. I especially like the topless—and top-heavy—masseuses.

•

Massage parlors are a great retreat for the tired and lonely businessman. Pleasure without obligation—except money of course.

•

Went to a topless bar the other day with some fellow workers. It was quite arousing. Don't think I'd have the nerve to ask the girl for sex, but I sure thought about it. I feel a little guilty about it. But what's the harm in just looking?

•

On Thursday or Friday afternoons when business is slow, a couple of guys at the office go to a topless bar down the street. In fact, the girls aren't wearing much on the bottom either. I meet one of the girls there for sex occasionally afterwards. Once I sucked a hickey on her boob so as to embarrass her at work. She's exciting to be with, and it turns me on to see her dance when a group of us goes to the bar.

•

On Friday afternoons, a couple of us go to topless dance places down the street. One girl especially has huge breasts with perky nipples. She stops by our table during breaks. I want to suck those nipples and fuck her. I often masturbate thinking of this. Plan to see if I can fulfill this fantasy.

I'm certainly still attractive and energetic, the 40-year-old argues. Maybe it's time to take my lusty feelings out of hock and re-oil the scoring mechanism. The other guys find pleasure in such epicurean delights. Maybe that's what's missing? Is this the mid-life crisis they've been telling me about? Mid-life crisis, that's what it's all about.

These men are for the most part the business and community leaders. Those 50 and older also comprise this power elite, but have reached their pinnacles and are winding down, focusing on retirement and security, or seriously reevaluating their last years at the helm.

Men in the 40s are in their occupational prime, still vital and energetic. As a group they represent the last bastion of America as it was before the counterculture revolution of the 1960s. They served patriotically in the Korean War and believed in the affluent technological solution to their own ills and the world's. They naively and determinedly pursued the good-life rewards of their executive sweat. As a group they didn't experience the cultural schism which divided the men who are now in their 30s.

They are almost to the top. And as "kings of the hill" they must fend off challenges—career women and younger men. Trying to keep their own power momentum, they resent being the scapegoats and targets of the cultural revolution. They feel they played the game fair and square, worked tirelessly, and deserve every reward obtainable.

Yet these men are sexually frustrated. They didn't totally buy the scoring and conquering they were taught, but since it was the only game in town, they played it the best they knew how. Now the games have kaleidoscoped. The rules have changed as have the players. Everyone is more open about sexuality (albeit in puritanical, self-conscious ways), women are more aggressive and sexually sure. However, these men sense more performance and achievement expectations placed upon them. In the past they indulged in grand stories of their "sexploits." Now that's not enough.

They're in a mid-life crisis and their sexuality is at the very core of it. Should they withdraw, change positions, or burrow deeper? They act out the virile male myth, knowing all the while that they hurt, have fears and uncertainties, and just plain want to be loved and understood. That's what the void's about.

The women of this era were not as "pure" as their forerunners, but they still remembered their place and still expected due reward for staying there. Usually high school sweethearts or college conquests, they hooked their men early. The underlying contract between the two, although never articulated in full, was this: we will fall in love, marry, raise a family, visit our in-laws over the holidays, and love, honor, and obey. Sex was children and love, and would work itself out with time, since she was inexperienced at first and he was unsure. She would feather the nest, decorate in Danish Modern or Colonial, and emotionally nurture her husband's success in the world and their children's accomplishments. He, in turn, would work long and hard.

Their sex life has never been that great; if it initially was, the novelty wore off long ago. But then that was part of the trade-off for stability. It wouldn't have been so bad if the new pressures to be sexually fulfilled hadn't started closing in. Now she wants something more and so does he. But won't that threaten the family bond and their intermittently renewed decision to stay together for the children's sake? Some try to spice up their own sex lives with new positions, new devices, new environments.

My wife and I have tried to renew and improve our sex life. At first this was difficult because we found that we had never really talked to each other about our sexual relationship. We started by reading and discussing some popular sex book (the *Joy of Sex* for instance) and magazines. We got up the nerve eventually to go together to buy her a vibrator and try that. We realize that we have much more to learn and to try with each other, but we are excited at the prospects. Interestingly, we can talk more openly about other subjects now, too.

•

I've been getting into being more romantic lately, and June, my wife, is really responding. Sounds crazy and like we're a couple of kids, but who cares. In fact, it's probably that our kids are now out of the house that we can do this. We dress up more often and go out to dinner. I bring June flowers just like when we were dating. After a good dinner and wine, we come home and make love. I even initiated our lovemaking once on the living-room sofa. She has bought some new negligees. All I can say is that I have never wanted to cheat on her, and if we can continue to add some zest in our sex life it is much better than me looking elsewhere. It takes some work, but so does anything that worthwhile.

Swapping spouses and participating in orgies are also fashionable options.

Several years ago I convinced my wife that we should try the swapping scene. I have heard some guys at work who do this and found out about some parties. She wouldn't do it for a long time. Finally when it was obvious that we either do that or I was going to go elsewhere for some sexual excitement, she said O.K. The first time was a disaster. She sat in the corner talking to some guy while I screwed his wife. The second time she had sex with this guy and even seemed to enjoy it. At first we'd discuss some things that went on in the sessions when we got home. But I've noticed it's a little tenser between us now. I don't know if she understands that this type of thing is for sexual novelty. She seems to enjoy her experiences, but might tend to get emotionally carried away.

They may try an "open marriage," temporarily perhaps shelving their monogamous ideals and deeply ingrained jealousies. Or they can mutually suffer in silence and sublimate their libidinous energies into P.T.A. meetings, longer work hours, and family ski trips.

I have occasional sexual fantasies during the day, but they're more the "flash in the pan" type because I'm so busy most of the time. To stay on top in business takes almost every ounce of a man's energy. You can usually tell a man who gets involved with someone. His work suffers.

•

I try to be as good a family man as I can. We have three great children, and I spend most weekends in family activities. Sure I have thoughts about sex with another woman, doesn't every man? Usually I set these thoughts in the back of my mind. It's hard enough to be a decent father and provider. I'm not superman, and my children come first in my life.

•

I have sexual fantasies occasionally during the day and also masturbatory fantasies. But I'm a religious man and don't let them get very far. I have thought about having sex with other women besides my wife but wouldn't because I consider it sinful.

Or they can go through the marital motions and look the other way as their partner pines for and perhaps pursues greener pastures.

My sexual fantasies usually all start with having seen some attractive behind or legs or breasts. I think it would be nice to have that person, and then the thought occurs to me that it would be nice to have lots of women in bed at the same time. I've never actually done this, but the thought is there. I think this thought several times a week. If I see a woman I'm attracted to (could be anywhere—street, office, what have you) I consider how I'd go about sleeping with her without my wife finding out about it and without feeling guilty about it. I think it's guilt that keeps me from sleeping with everybody I've ever had a fantasy about.

Sometimes the wife, in her stifling environment, has turned into a desperate bitch. The money isn't coming in fast enough, the life she sacrificed for isn't so great, the children are grown and going off on their own. Daughter seems to be doing things mother only dreamed about—career, independence, adventure. The "little woman" might give it a desperate try—reading and re-reading *Cosmopolitan* and *The Total Woman* for the sure solution to marital bliss and how to keep the husband she nabbed in her more alluring days. After all, she is told, she was over the hill when she hit 30.

The other night my wife met me at the door dressed in a sexy outfit, and we had a delicious dinner alone (children were at their grandmother's) and made love afterward. It was great. I wish she would make the effort more often. She usually doesn't seem very into sex.

•

My wife read *The Total Woman* and is trying real hard to be sexy to me. I appreciate her efforts and concern, and I love her. But let's face it. After twenty-two years—with someone who didn't even seem to like sex most of the time—just because she wears a see-through nightie, I can't automatically turn into a bull with her.

Sadly, the unattained conjugal closeness and enjoyment are only a symbolic part of the larger problem—they haven't really communicated in years. Their marital masquerade concealed frustrations, fears, and hurts. Resentment and anger bubbled through but the real issues weren't exposed. It's become difficult to take off the marital masks. Besides, what is underneath would demand new expressions and behavior. Better to leave well enough alone. But the male in his 40s feels restless and unfulfilled. Where can he go?

He can go to a prostitute to receive momentary release and consolation. His generation is not unfamiliar with this woman; he might well have been initiated into manhood by her, or might have gone to her to soothe his loneliness while a soldier overseas.

Having been trained to degrade their partner as a sexual object and segregate lust from love, a number of men at this age go to prostitutes for their sexual enjoyment. They enjoy the clandestine, illicit aspects and being in control of their "sexploit." Instead of wasting valuable time, they prefer the instant and desired satisfaction they can direct the prostitute to provide. Many of these men have for years gone to prostitutes for the kinkier sex that they'd never share with their wives. Until recently, even oral sex was for them a forbidden pleasure. And certainly out-of-town junkets could be relieved of some loneliness and libidinal build-up by pay-as-you-come sex.

I fantasize ravishing a prostitute—paying her to do all the things I've wanted in sex. Sucking me till I go dry; putting her tongue in my rectum; doing a striptease and taunting me with her cunt. Every once in a while I pick one up when I'm out of town, but I've never had one do all these things I'd like.

•

I enjoy being set up—by some business that wants a contract with us—on a night on the town. This usually involves bringing in attractive girls that join us at dinner and one that will be mine for the night. There are some real winners. I like to discreetly play with my "date" during dinner. Often these "dates" are quite intelligent and know their way around. Some are even college graduates who make a lot of money this way. Sometimes I enjoy my talks after sex with them as much as the sex itself. They often seem to understand me and are good company in an otherwise cold and lonely situation. I have a "regular" in Tucson that's up for me each time I come to town. She's a blond barmaid that is sort of a grown-up flower child. I look forward to my times with her. In addition to her other attributes, she gives fantastic head.

•

I don't know why. Maybe it's because of the fraternity outings to Nevada to houses of prostitution which were so exciting years ago. I just know that I enjoy getting together with a small group of guys and picking up some women of the night. Besides the sex there is some kind of group excitement and manly closeness in doing this, if you know what I mean. Last time, one guy and I decided to take our girls to the same room and traded off at half time. The girls seemed to like that too. It was a turn-on to see my friend and one of the girls fucking in the next bed. Would like to try more group-type sex. It's very stimulating. I think of the combinations and permutations of male-female sex as I masturbate sometimes.

•

The only way I can really get off is by having sex with a hooker. I do this whenever I travel out of town.

His peers, and predecessors, often focus their sexual energies on the "pretty young things" at the office or at the singles bars. He feels most comfortable, yet a bit silly, in the pursuit of these trophies. They massage his ego—and whatever else—and make him feel that he isn't such a bad guy after all. Besides actual encounters, he keeps the juices flowing with fantasies. He livens otherwise boring meetings by "mentally undressing" and seducing the attractive women around.

This man is especially vulnerable to the poised, independent career woman ten or fifteen years his junior. He is immensely attracted by her intelligence and ambition. He feels safe that she's not out to syphon his status and money, yet his fascination and attraction is complemented by a fear of this unknown entity. He can very easily fall for her because she comes as such a surprise.

After an intense exchange with this "bright young woman" he may feel that he's finally found his match.

Mickey and I met at a conference in Chicago. She's a sales representative from our West Coast subsidiary. Since then we've met whenever we can and the relationship has been a wonderful one. I've never enjoyed sex more with anyone. She understands much of my hassles in business and even shares some. All she asks from me is my presence and love and accepts me for what I am. Sometimes I feel torn between her and my family, though I think it's more my conflict than one imposed by her. I miss her deeply when we're apart and find myself wishing I'd met someone like her twenty-five years ago. When I masturbate I fantasize making love with her. Sex is an adventure with her and we explore and fulfill together. Sometimes in our separation I think of new experiences we can have, and we talk about them over the phone. These hot long-distance conversations turn us both on and often end in masturbation.

Dissatisfied with the shallowness of his life, he is excitedly drawn to the magnificent blending of mind and body he has found. Paradoxically, his encounter with this liberated woman is simultaneously a glimpse of his own liberated potential, so he may fantasize her as the goddess she isn't. He will attribute to her all the qualities found lacking in the women previously so important in his life. In his infatuation, he will mythologize and delude himself. But as rapidly as he reached his dreamy, infatuated peak, he'll start feeling threatened by this new woman and resentful that she doesn't really emulate his dreams. They'll have an intense but tentative affair. He may discard his family or even his lifestyle for this new woman. But the initial relief that she doesn't want to smother him or to live vicariously through his position can soon turn to panic as he realizes she doesn't *need* him to provide the traditional supports. The original excitement in their mutual enjoyment can turn into a feeling of one more burden in his life as he tries constantly to fulfill her sexually and prove he's the greatest lover around. He wants to be needed and loved for himself—not just for his penis. Suddenly he has a sense of what it might mean to be treated as a sexual object. The acceptance and safe haven he thought he had bring new complications.

Very often he heals his injured ego by turning to the idolizing office groupies who beg for his attentions. They tend to be nonambitious, insecure young women who crave older masculine guidance and assurance. Quick to laugh indiscriminately at his every joke and shower him with obsequious attentions, they help restore his much maligned image and faith in himself.

He courts these groupies, all the time at a safe emotional distance. He needs them but provides no meaningful dialogue beyond a fatherly love-crumb of reinforcement.

Meanwhile he settles for brief affairs and adventures to provide spots of emotional light in his otherwise routine existence. He joins his colleagues in "convention fever," stalking willing prey on out-of-town junkets.

I went to San Diego for a conference last week, so far from home and the elders of the church. The girls were young and sexy and I was constantly horny. The first night a bunch of us sat in the bar, and as we got drunker one of the girls sitting next to me looked like she was ready. My penis was harder than it had been in a long time. After a while most of the people left the table. She was still there, looking better all the time. I put my hand casually and quickly on her thigh one time, and she didn't seem to mind. We ordered another drink, and then I suggested we go to my room for a drink. She was tottering a bit by now, and I couldn't wait to get her alone. She said O.K. and I felt like a teenager. Unfortunately we'd both had too much to drink and staggered a little on our way up to my room. When we got in the door I started feeling her body before we had even completely closed the door. She was ready, but a bit unstable. I rubbed her breasts and undressed her as I was also getting out of my clothes. We fell on the bed. I pushed my penis in her mouth, she sucked me so good I almost came. Too much alcohol meant that when I entered her I wasn't as hard as before and didn't last very long. I think about that convention many times when I masturbate and enlarge upon the facts. I fantasize screwing her from every position conceivable—even in her ass and she screams how good it is. She thinks (in my fantasy of course) that I'm the best man she's been with and wants me all the time. She begs me for more and wants to be my mistress. She sucks my penis and does anything I want. This fantasy gets more exciting with time. Now I can't wait for the next conference and what might occur.

•

New Orleans is the place for a good time. Recently I went to a convention there. Bourbon Street is alive, and people seem to go with the trend. I met one of my colleagues from another state whom I hadn't really known before. After the last meeting we ventured to dinner together. Then we decided to check out some of the topless shows—just sort of out of curiosity. Some of the shows were not so terrific, but others were a turn-on, especially after a few drinks. I could sense that Helen was getting turned on too. Finally, we made it back to the hotel, and I walked her to her room. I went in with her and shut the door quickly. She was hot, we undressed as fast as we could with little foreplay and just got to it. Her vagina was hot and sucked me in. Never had such a feeling. We hungrily fucked each other till we were both exhausted. The next two nights we did the same and have arranged to meet at a regional conference in the fall. I've been dreaming about what we'll do and get excited by the prospects. Generally I lead a routine life and am very busy at work. Can't wait for our meeting. I daydream often about it and even masturbate thinking about her. She's not so attractive but really wants sex, and that gets me going. When I read *Playboy,* I plan what we'll do the next time we meet. Sure livens up another routine day.

He fantasizes, discreetly grabs a few skirts at work, and may even experiment more fervently in the vast potpourri of credit-card sex, Roman baths, and anonymous group-sex encounters. All safe, quick, and lusty. As he planes from place to place, he has sexual fantasies about the flight attendants which he may try to fulfill, although some magic seems to be lost in the landing.

Having denied his feeling so long, he contemplates his relationship with his aging mother. Dimensions increase as he analyzes his caring and his carefully repressed sexual responses to his daughters, who have become young women overnight.

He knows there is much going on inside him but doesn't know what to do about it. Is it best to channel his sexual energies into one-night stands? Where can he unload his hurt? Who will provide solutions? Who will understand?

Too many people act like the physical part of sex is all a man needs. A one-night affair might relieve momentary horniness, but a steady diet of these one-nighters can be unfulfilling and lonely if there isn't anyone around to love.

•

One thing women don't understand about us men is that we have feelings, too. Just because we don't cry all the time doesn't mean things are easy or that we don't get hurt.

•

I fantasize about being held all the time, especially after an orgasm. If given the opportunity I would love to experience in reality the fantasy of tenderness and love.

The prostitute, his independent mistress, the groupie, or his one-night stand provides her own solace and does listen at least and love him a little. He could never share his real feelings with his mother; he resents her for setting him onto her traditional idea of a proper life's course unprepared for its consequences. For his wife, he has always had to play the strong role—she would crumble if his strong exterior appeared cracked. She doesn't have to deal with the cruel outside world; she doesn't know what it is. They stopped talking years ago anyway.

You always hear the cliché "My wife doesn't understand me." But it's often true. I love my wife, but I find I have to brace myself before walking in that door at night to deal with her complaints. I know things aren't great for her, but who can I complain to? She won't really listen. Besides, how can she understand my frustrations at work? How can she understand how I get sick of playing the sales game? Sometimes I think if the boss sends me to take one more group of out-of-town contractors to lunch, I'll smash somebody. How can a man get into being romantic or even care, when he's got those constant problems?

He has a strange intuition that his daughter, despite her youth and lack of experience, understands at a subconscious, visceral level what he is about. But he can't talk to her about such outlandish things; in fact, he has trouble even knowing how to be her father.

He certainly can't go to any man about his dilemma. The American male knows he can't share deep feelings with another of his sex—that's unmanly. He can't go to his peers, though he suspects many are sharing his crisis. He can't go to older men, for he has always been their challenger. Nor can he go to the younger men, who are obviously his juniors. They won't understand, and even if he could communicate with them he would surely lose his credibility and dominant position. He longs to warn his son of this impending doom, but what can he say? Maybe he should go to a shrink, but that constitutes an admission of weakness.

So he holds his pain and confusion deep inside and tries to act as if it is of little consequence. He jokes with the guys, tries to enjoy his private thoughts and special moments and not be too concerned with all that he is feeling.

To spice up their lives, the mid-lifers fantasize. To prepare for new experience, they dream. There are fantasies which are popular with these men.

Sex with two or more women ranks number one. Most of these men have wondered what several women in bed would be like. If one woman is a turn-on, two women must be twice as stimulating, and more women would add even greater sexual possibilities, provoking continuous erections and rapid-fire orgasms.

I imagine a dozen seductive, exciting women turning me on, from one orgasm to another.

Sometimes they want to have the women interact sexually with each other. It's a turn-on for many men to watch women making love. Feminine emotional depth and tenderness attract men who feel that they can't allow themselves to express such feelings. Some men incorporate their wives into the fantasy. This can expand the sexual experiences of both, but in a togetherness that somehow legitimizes the *ménage à trois* and brings man and wife closer together than they have been for a long time. The man can also vicariously take the part of the other woman as she excites his wife and shares with her the tender, sensitive caresses he would like to give.

A number of men in their 40s are aroused by thinking of their wives or lovers having sex with another man. This other man is a stud, the James Bond he aspires to be in his Walter Mitty daydreams. The other man drives his wife wild just as he has always wanted to do. He sees his "Snow White" spouse awaken to a sexuality unknown to them in their puritanical marriage, and he thrives on her wanton sensuality.

Such a fantasy can also provide a screen for homosexual feelings. It is normal for all men and women to have occasional thoughts of caressing or having sex with someone of their own sex, but it is very difficult for the man of traditional American mores to accept such thoughts. So he can now see another aroused man, note sexual skills, and vicariously take his wife's role in the action without feeling repulsed or ashamed of his own homosexual interest or fleeting desires. Once again the presence of his wife legitimizes any desires he would normally find unacceptable. It is only right that she should be a part of his fantasy life just as she is part of his real life.

Elaborating upon such fantasies, the male creates more complicated sexual combinations. His wife (or lover) might be present. Besides enjoying rapid-fire orgasms with many women, he can enjoy watching others and fulfill some of his voyeuristic urges. He can also look around the cabal to see if there are any new tricks or treats to add to his sexual repertoire.

I fantasize about participating in an orgy. My wife and I attend this party. The wine is flowing. Some woman starts stripteasing to the music. Soon couples are screwing and swapping and screwing again. I look across the room and see another man putting his cock into my wife. Two women are caressing me and one starts giving me head. I have sex with one, then go on to the other. Wild!

Clandestine affairs are very exciting to think about and to have. They are the forbidden, perhaps dangerous, encounters which add thrills to a normally routine existence. These fantasies are frequent and may include a brief and hurried moment with a neighbor before her husband returns, seduction of a flight attendant in a crowded plane, or a quick fling with a colleague behind office doors while unsuspecting secretaries type away outside the door. The possibilities are unlimited. The potential danger and prospect of being caught is the stimulus, not unlike first swipes at sex as a kid.

I am giving the beautiful nurse next door driving lessons. (She's married to an older man and is a good friend of my wife's.) The second day of the lesson, I move my hand to help her steer, then put my hand on her voluptuous breasts. Soon we've pulled over in the woods and are making love.

Psychoanalytic theory purports that we all have sexual fantasies about our fathers, mothers, sisters, and brothers, because we are close to them in growing up. We are sexual beings before we even emerge from the womb. Societal taboos against incest, however, force us to repress sexual thoughts and desires involving other family members. But the urges remain and emerge in nonthreatening ways. Our man of 40 might fantasize sex with his own mother, but more likely she will be generalized and transformed into *a mother*. He might fantasize sex with his own daughter, but more likely with *a daughter* and her mother. Again he has his two women who symbolize in their ways the important females in his life—his mother, his daughter, and his daughter's mother.

I love to think about having sex with a mother-daughter team. They're both beautiful. The mother is experienced and warm, the daughter just learning and tight. I go from one to the other till we all collapse in exhaustion.

He often fantasizes about a younger woman. For it is exciting to seduce and teach her, to feel her warm lithe body and the sense of youthfulness she restores to his life. Women, too, have fantasies of sex with younger men or boys. The only difference is they do not act upon them with the ease of their male counterparts.

I know it's not practical, but I see these young things walking down the street, and I want to pick up one of those Lolitas, undress her, and show her how she should be made love to.

Also common to men in their 40s are fantasies of dominating a woman in sex, or of being themselves submissive in an encounter.

I want to dominate my girlfriend—to have her beg me for attention, for sex. Then I coldly tell her to strip and stoop over on the rug and wait for me. She begs me to enter her. I finally do and bang her so hard she screams and begs me for more.

•

I have fantasies of my lover standing above me. I try to stand to reach her, but she firmly pushes me back down. She makes me grovel and crawl before she consents to have sex. Then I massage her and eat her until she's ready to let me penetrate. When I get in after waiting and trying so long, I explode with pleasure.

We all have a mixture of sadistic and masochistic urges, one of which can be the major influence in a person's sexual fantasies and behavior. Or else it may color one's behavior and thoughts in an individual moment, sometimes depending on whom one is with and in what setting. But more commonly we are subject to the intermittent influences of both sadistic and masochistic urges so that in one situation we may wish to dominate and in another we may want to be dominated. The male in mid-life seems to give freer rein to these influences in order to add new dimensions to his routine. He allows his fantasies to become more elaborate at a more conscious level, often previewing them quite deliberately. No longer are they flashes for he now allows himself to actually create and savor his fantasy inventions.

Oral Sex

Since it has become more accepted and better publicized, our man is especially interested in oral sex.

> When I masturbate I close my eyes and envision a beautiful woman with flowing long hair. She takes my penis in her mouth, licks, sucks, and tantalizes it —then she puts it deep in her throat and I come.

He likes the very good feeling it gives him, and fantasies of having fellatio performed on him are far more frequent and important to him than thoughts of his carrying out oral sex on women, but he does participate in the latter. More interested in foreplay than he was twenty years ago, he feels more obligation to prepare his partner through precoital play because he's concerned about her receptivity and her pleasure. In the old days, he just wanted her to be wet enough for his penetration. Now he wants to drive her wild with precoital titillation and concentrates more on the overture. Besides, having one's penis sucked is very pleasurable. Movies like *Deep Throat* inspire variations.

Oral desires of the 40-year-old male also involve women's breasts, where, of course, the desire started in the first place. He is turned on by women's breasts, usually the big maternal ones which *Playboy* has extolled for years. Hard nipples seen through soft blouses excite him. He wants to feel and caress and suck these feminine protrusions. While his counterparts in other cultures find other parts of the female anatomy to be a more direct turn-on, he is still a "breast man" first.

The sexual behavior and erotic yearnings of these men fall within the context of what they've been taught sex is about, their attitudes and experiences with women, their fear of homosexuality, and a stark awareness that they aren't getting any younger.

5

The Throbbing Thirties

Still throbbing with a cultural hangover, these men stop in the midst of their busy drop-in or unbusy drop-out schedules to evaluate and reevaluate the direction of their lives. The counterculture revolution of the sixties produced two main groups of young men: the drop-ins—who brushed aside much of the social conflict and went on about the business of their predecessors; and the drop-outs—who tried to shed their cultural heritage and find out what individual essence resided underneath, to discover what for them would be truly "meaningful" and "relevant." The former resolved to go up in the world, the latter to get "high" and find another life.

THE DROP-IN

Having reached his first plateau of success in the seventies, the drop-in is looking below and around him. Is up the way to go and what has been sacrificed in the climb already? He didn't join his college buddies in Haight-Ashbury. If he couldn't muster an education deferment, he steeled himself and went to Vietnam for the mandatory stint. He followed the American success guide to the letter. After getting the M.B.A. or law degree, he's doing well in business. Promotions abound. Wife is managing the children and home affairs as she should and driving the suburban station wagon. She's even taking "courses" so she can stay interesting, and working part time so she can associate a bit with the outside world. But she's become boring. He can't talk with her about what's important to him; he sees his associates and the mailman eying her hungrily.

I've had affairs outside of my marriage. They were O.K. My concern now is enjoying sex more and somehow figuring out how to liven up my marriage. The last year my wife and I have been distant. I've also been concerned about performing sexually. Always wondered about how the size of my penis compared to other men. I suppose I'm adequate. But recently I've had incidents of impotence with her and in some affairs. Then it really disturbed me when my wife admitted having a three-month affair with one of the workers at our house. (This was her first big affair as far as I know.) She said she won't see him again and I believe her. But I think she enjoyed sex with him more than she ever did with me. The damage has been done.

She's a mandatorily beautiful and sexy woman, and he must satisfy her so she won't stray. He needs her to hold the dream together. But how can they make things better? Maybe a vacation apart will help, or a marriage counselor, or a vacation together. Maybe if he jogs more regularly or bashes the hell out of the tennis ball things will work themselves out. He just can't handle ten more years like the last.

I enjoy my family and my job. I enjoy sex with my wife and love her very much. As well as things are going, I also know I need a change. Just haven't decided what or how.

•

I'm very successful in my job and have a good family. At first I said to myself that I had fulfilled well all the goals I set for myself in college. I started brewing up new goals and new challenges, but had a haunting feeling inside that new goals aren't the answer. They wouldn't necessarily provide the change I need or the fulfillment I feel is lacking. I don't know what to do, but I have a feeling it should somehow be more along the lines of pulling away from the goals and structures and the things expected from a man. I want to be happy and be good to myself. I feel I'm locked into accomplishing goals and not enjoying me and other people.

The office affairs added some spice, but the parties aren't as much fun as they used to be. The competing career women offer some homage and chance for understanding dialogues mixed with sexual vibrations. But he has to watch it. They can get awfully smart and awfully pushy. With women's lib in vogue, they might even be competing for his job. And they don't have families to worry about or wives to keep content. They can strike out independently in any direction. He resents their freedom, their inflated income, and their overachieving persistence. Some are too serious and too angry. Probably need to have sex more often or have a child. Others are charming and damn good at their jobs. Too good.

I think about kissing, touching, and making love to women who work for me at the bank. Typically we go to her apartment after dinner or drinks. . . . I am very aroused—very hard and therefore very satisfying for the woman who believes I am a great lover.

•

Julie, one of the young women executives in the office, is beautiful as well as bright. I have fantasies of seducing her, of making love till neither of us can move. Bet she's a good lover—she has a lot of sensual energy.

•

I would like to make love to two lesbians who would, of course, be loving each other. It is quite a turn-on to see two women having sex with each other. I suppose it is exciting to see their reciprocation of tenderness and emotion.

•

I think about what it would be like to make love with a man. Mostly I fantasize this when I've had a little to drink, and am masturbating. Cold sober this thought is repulsive.

•

I want to tie a woman down on the bed and screw her unmercifully like in *The Story of O*. I want her to beg me for more, and I'll give it to her only when I want to.

•

When I'm on trips I call my girlfriend at night. Eventually we end up sharing sexy thoughts and masturbating. I then proceed to good dreams and restful sleep.

•

A woman I know in San Francisco is uninhibited in her sex life. Often we masturbate as we talk on the phone. Once when I called she was in bed with another guy. The thought turned me on. She consented to my request and gave me a "blow by blow" account of their activities.

•

I come into a room with wall-to-wall carpeting—there are three women on three different beds, all have on black panties—one woman Black, two white—go to Black woman; take her pants down slowly; have one of other women come over to bed;

she spreads her cheeks—plays with her—lubricates her anus; other woman on her knees—takes down pants, spreads legs; I fuck one while one sucks the other.

●

I'd like to do something far-out sexually, like having group sex—an orgy—or something. At our college fraternity we used to have a wild Roman orgy party and invite the wild girls we knew. I'd like to do something like this again, but really go all the way where everyone could be fucking all around and trading off. Guess I feel I need some diversity from the routine of work and the "model" family.

●

A Black woman I work with is extremely sexy. We've never had sex, but I think she might also be interested. I fantasize about her constantly, especially after we've talked. I imagine I casually rub her enormous breasts and she responds. We lock my office door and make love on my plush orange carpet. She's a very sensual woman and I know it'd be an exciting encounter. Maybe I should stop fantasizing and give it a try.

●

Sharon is a woman executive in our company. She's brilliant and good-looking too. We've had some good talks, and I feel a lot of sexual attraction between us. I often fantasize making love to her. We are working late one night and somehow end up in each other's arms. We make passionate love. I don't know why I've hesitated so long about approaching her for this. Guess I'm not quite sure how to. She is also living with this Black fellow.

●

I don't have specific "daydream," "masturbatory," or "relations" fantasies. Rather, I experience the same general fantasies during all three. I don't know if they are fantasies so much as they are recollections: I enjoy remembering experiences I have had with different girls, one in particular. She was the first girl I ever screwed, and she had, to me, the perfect figure—large breasts, rather heavy (but not fat) legs, small feet, short (five feet two). I was 15 at the time. She had a profound impact on my sex life. Since then, I compare all girls, all figures, to hers. She is in most of my sexual fantasies, and I suppose some of them truly are fantasies, since I imagine us in situations (she with nothing but nylons on while we're making love) that we never actually experienced. I am a foot fetishist, which I attribute mainly to her (although I can recall those urges prior to meeting her). High spike heels were the vogue then, and I am still excited by them. When I recall my old girls, I always put them in high heels.

•

Most of my fantasies are recollections, exactly as I can remember them, of actual experiences I enjoyed with that first girl: in her bedroom (me on top, her on top), in her bathtub (not both of us—she takes a bath, I watch), she bouncing her breasts in front of a mirror (she was darn near an exhibitionist, or maybe she was fascinated—I certainly was—that a 15-year-old body could be so totally developed). When I masturbate, I recall various girls, but 99 percent of the time, when I climax, my mind is on her.

•

I masturbate to the thoughts of past sexual encounters or a group sex scene where I am the only male. A mother and daughter relationship where both are competing for my affections and both win is also very stimulating.

THE DROP-OUT

We are walking hand in hand in the mountains (with meadows and plains). We have not seen any people.

I hold her close, and we begin to undress each other slowly. We engage in oral genital sex (69) and reach climax at the same time. We move apart feeling the sun and soft grass on our bodies although we are still touching each other lightly. We move back together alternating between myself on top and her on top until pleasantly exhausted. This fantasy also takes place in my home to soft music after a good meal which I have cooked.

Abbie Hoffman, where are you now that I need you? Tom Hayden, what happened to that new world you promised? Eldridge Cleaver, how could you? Anger of the sixties at the core, apathy of the seventies creeping in from the sides, the drop-out has said good-bye to Thoreau's and to B. F. Skinner's Waldens and returned to the margins of the establishment to make ends meet. After ten years, acid trips, and some bouts with utopian attempts, the drop-out is dropping in a bit. Economic survival, disillusionment, and mellowing promote return.

Six to ten years ago, I occasionally pursued the object of daydream fantasy in order to actualize the fantasy. More recently, I have not done so because of my developed consciousness surrounding the interrelation of physical/emotional feelings. I was, in the past, not willing to relate to many of the women I slept with, being interested primarily in a sexual experience. I am no longer able to be as careless and carefree about sexual experiences as I once was.

•

Sometimes in the middle of a daydream fantasy generated by simply seeing an attractive woman, I criticize myself for the objectification and stop the fantasy.

Looking for a satisfactory re-entry style, he consorts with former lovers and wives, enrolls the children in school, and works to find the cultural golden mean which will safeguard his integrity while paying the bills. He has lost valuable time in the business world, while establishment buddies and ambitious female classmates have moved ahead in the rat race.

On his Siddharthan sojourn he met life in its many forms. Expanding his mind and extending his emotions with drugs, he broke down—at least superficially—many of the puritanical confines of his upbringing.

As an extremely regular rule when masturbating, I focus on a woman I know and to whom I feel sexually attracted. My focus is on her, naked, and moves from the general to the specific where I am sucking her breasts (large nipples are right-on) or my mouth is buried in her cunt (lots of hair sometimes is a turn-on) or her sucking my penis. Sometimes the place is not well defined. I guess in bed; less frequently rolling in the grass. Or even less frequently, in some sort of warm, shallow tub or pool. Eight to twelve years ago I occasionally masturbated looking at *Playboy*. Currently, three or four times a year I may use an erotic magazine for arousal—maybe less.

•

The women I use for my masturbating fantasies are mostly in my age group (20–35 years old) or women I know. Occasionally, rarely, an older woman or younger woman might be the object.

•

I'm more into having a really good relationship these days. I feel that I am somewhat trapped by stereotypes—would have trouble being romantically intimate with a fat woman, etc. I've been masturbating considerably less than I used to, which I think parallels a certain withdrawal from intimacy in general.

As he looked to the East for answers and ways, he dealt more directly with his sexuality. He tried sex with different women, in groups, sometimes even with men. He went without sex. He watched others in sex and measured himself against the men. He watched women together. He opened himself to more tenderness, sharing his most intimate thoughts and dreams.

He broke out of his cultural classification to mix with those of other ethnic groups. He set his college degree on the bench to cut wood with the worker. Women became his friends. He became his own friend. Where could he go with his new self in the old world?

The woman in my fantasies is small, slim, with large breasts, brown or black hair, kind, self-reliant, not wanting a father figure, not wanting a male to baby, interested in art, socialist politics, camping—a stable individual not into unnecessary game playing.

There is no one answer to be found for *him* in the great books or from the great gurus. He looks to others for comfort, with the deep-down realization of the loneliness of being a cultural pioneer. His baptism of fire made him a more sensitive creature. He's relieved and feels more like a person than a John Wayne poster. But he must still forge solutions. Glimpses of some universals in drug-induced states have left him expanded but dissatisfied. How can he turn his survival stress—the struggle for the "survival of his integrity"—into creative tension?

He looks with envy and a bit of haughtiness upon those in their 20s who have, at least superficially, seemed to minimize the social conflict and mold fragments of traditional and new to create a comfortable cultural quilt.

He knows women better than he once did. He explores relationships with women of diverse ages, from many backgrounds and creeds. He now feels comfortable with the tenderness of his partner, for he has accepted the tenderness within himself.

Some of my fantasies during orgasm are euphoric and abstract—like rushing through space with no feeling of time or direction, or seeing exploding colors or fireworks.

The special experiences he's had in his sexuality make him discriminating. He may have sex frequently but he is satisfied only with that deep encounter—the sexual means to reaching the cosmos in himself. He knows this is a rarity but settles for little less.

As he drops back in, the first score he must settle is with his mother. He must somehow deal with his mixture of guilt, anger, and deep love for her. It is confusing. To allow her to touch him he must go against the cultural ways he's been taught. He thinks he can now show her the love and friendship he kept so guarded—especially from her. At least he can show the tolerance. At least he can release the tears.

He can now go to his father and understand. They can smoke the emotional pipe of peace and laugh together and look each other straight in the eye—and at life and destiny.

He can love his woman, daughter, and son with abandon. He is afraid. But that's all right because he knows he's alive.

Sex with two or more women is a fantasy popular among men from their late 20s to their 50s. This fantasy symbolizes their aspirations for power and achievement. Knowing well their personal physical limitations, they look to this bacchanalian delight to free them from realistic constraints.

I have always fantasized making it with two or three women at the same time. Don't know if I could fulfill them all, but I'd sure as hell try.

•

I have fantasies of having sex with several women at once. It might increase my sex capabilities. With all those women, I might have multi-orgasms—I'd enjoy with them that rapid-fire repeat-action sex.

More than the 40s group, men in their 30s are fascinated by the relationship and erotic affection of the women in the threesome. Comfortable and even a bit bored with traditional sexual positions and ways, these men want to explore with their partners new possibilities. They have fantasies of sex on horseback, special devices, and even new mating positions which they are sure have never been tried.

I asked one woman I was with to use her vibrator for me. It was a real turn-on to watch her masturbate with it. I've been fantasizing using it on her next time we're together.

They explore in reality and fantasy the art of massage.

I bought a shower massager the other day, plan to use it on Susan when she comes to stay this weekend.

They enjoy the creative, adventuresome women who will accompany them in this exploration, and they look to innovative books and movies to offer new approaches to an ancient ritual.
They stock their pantries with strawberry preserves and whipped cream as they fantasize new places and new ways.

Heard from a friend that toothpaste is a stimulating thing to put on your penis head or the woman's clitoris. Last night I put some on and it *was* stimulating. I then masturbated while thinking of putting it on my girlfriend and sucking it off.

Reuniting lovemaking with nature, they fantasize seductions on the beach, making love in meadows, and ecstasy on the cliffs of Yosemite.

I'm a romantic at heart; would love to seduce a woman in the moonlight on the beach—and make love in the water as waves smash against us.

In their endeavors to relate to their partners and become more total men, unafraid of caring and emotion, they extend totality of expression to an awareness of special times and places. In letting themselves go in making love, they even orgasm to the harmony of nature.

When I make love with a woman I'm really into sometimes experiencing a vivid vision of abstract paintings, rushing water, or the flowing of natural forces.

The drop-ins are especially turned on by fantasizing and acting out hidden, dangerous, but emotionally safe affairs. Playing the straight life on the public stage, they grasp for more exciting pleasures behind the curtains.

Martha comes in from her company for a ten o'clock meeting. I ask her to close my office door. As she starts to sit down I go to her and start fondling her breasts. She resists at first—afraid we'll be discovered—but succumbs as we make love on my couch.

Married women seem to pose a special challenge.

I don't know why but much of my fantasy life is centered around seducing and having a secret affair with a married woman. Sometimes I have a certain person in mind, but more often not. I just think the idea of making love with a woman who's married is like wanting a forbidden fruit—she's taken, but I can persuade her to be with me—sort of a power trip I suppose.

The drop-ins are following their drop-out counterparts in attempting more meaningful dialogues with their partners. Relating to the person they're loving is more important than it was, even if it's an existential one-day, one-hour, no-expectations sort of intimacy.

I'm getting tired of sport fucking, if you don't mind. Gets kind of empty after a while. While I'm not ready to get tied down I do want more meaning when I'm in bed.

These men fantasize about women they know and have been involved with or would like to be. No faceless bodies for them. No prostitutes that go bump in the night, then fade back into anonymity. They want to relate in more delicate ways than before. They want to know women and yearn to better know themselves.

6

The Mellow Twenties

Ask someone in his 20s and he'll say he's chosen the best of both worlds—the world of the traditional American male and that of the counterculturalist.

Unlike his traditional senior, he relates to women as friends first. Experimenting with life and sexual possibilities in his college and early professional years, he intends to find his niche eventually.

It's funny, but I have very few fantasies during genital sex. I don't consider myself a great lover so most of my thoughts are on concentrating on the needs of my partner. I still have a tendency to have what I consider premature ejaculation so I feel that I use the oral sex as a supplement. If it seems as though I can't control my ejaculation so as to ensure my partner's pleasure, I will perform any other type of activity desired. I don't consider any type of hetero-sexual fetishes weird, and I really get off on using sex devices. This is probably due to a feeling of inadequacy on my part. I'm not ashamed of coming early, but I do want my partner to be satisfied the majority of the time.

But he and his women friends are more realistic about their future careers and life-styles than their predecessors—and often significantly less committed. He grew up in a permissive society and the turmoil of the 1960s. Lacking a structual rigidity in his upbringing and a dire, continuing threat to his survival, such as a war or a depression, he lacks the survival tension familiar to his predecessors. He grew up in relatively affluent surroundings, and his greatest problem is that of unlimited possibilities for his life-style. He doesn't feel a compulsion eventually to provide for his mate or marry right out of college. He may be involved with a person in another town or even living with someone, but sexual exclusivity is not necessarily an overriding part of the relationship. He understands the practicality of a good job, but wants one that is relatively interesting and personally satisfying. Unless he has gone the way of the fanatic cultists (fleeing from the discomfort of choosing possibilities and escaping instead into a haven of dogma, structure, and supermeaning otherwise absent in his formative years), he commits himself tentatively and tenuously. He believes that feelings are important in men as well as women, and that intelligence, sexual inclination, and active involvement in life are important in women as well as men.

My sexual feelings are almost always accompanied with feelings of "real" love, i.e.—it isn't just a sexual seduction scene. The women are not strangers.

•

During sex I think of my girlfriend and me as whole spiritual free beings of choice to copulate and consume the world in love wherever they may find the occasion.

•

When I masturbate, I concentrate on the intense emotional or physical yearning the fantasy woman and I have for each other. Often while we fuck we stare deeply into each other's eyes (something I haven't yet encountered in real sex and would like to have).

As a member of a new culture he is amazingly comfortable in his unheralded experimentation while aware of the possible toll demanded. He and his friends of both sexes exorcise some of their apprehensions in their tribal rituals—smoking marijuana, philosophizing, and sometimes sharing feelings.

He willingly maintains a facade regarding business. Not feeling that he's discarding his personal integrity, he doesn't mind wearing the three-piece suit to the office. He agrees to play the "degree" game, but does not take it very seriously. In his private life he's the counterculturalist—rapping, smoking dope, polygamous in his involvements until he decides to marry. He's not so threatened as his elders by bisexual or homosexual experiments and tendencies.

I've pondered homosexual activity as a recipient during daydreams but have never experienced it.

More important to him is relating to the "total person" and disposing of destructive hypocrisies of the past.

He has his fears as well. Emergence of the "new woman" has left everyone a little scared (including her). Some of his male friends retreat from the new-culture rules and activities. They have enough to learn about sex or life without having to contend with being stalked by interested females. Or he may learn to enjoy such attention.

When I masturbate I fantasize I am in some way restrained (and often standing) so I cannot move, but am very exposed. A parade of women, either that I know and like or have recently seen, come by each

121

in turn (though sometimes in groups) exciting me sexually by fondling and kissing until finally I am into one of them and come. The last one is generally the one I'm involved with or enamored of. Sometimes the women are competing to see who excites me the most.

He may openly date older women (a fantasy common to younger men but one strongly criticized by society in its actualization). In fact, he may find himself involved with that 30-year-old woman who has just severed a hectic relationship with one of his father's peers. A source of puzzlement to older men, he exhibits enormous ease in his relationships with women and other men.

After living together intermittently with several people, he may decide to marry. But he and his wife will view matrimony in the realistic terms of the times—planning to give it a strong try, but vowing not to be crushed if things don't work out. They have less at stake in this contract than their parents did. Traditional sex roles will be replaced by individual roles.

He is confused but generally able to make necessary adjustments. He is a man of two worlds; it isn't always easy.

My number one sexual fantasy is hitting a home run in Fenway Park, preferably against the Yankees. Mind you, this is from someone who in little league batted .083. As far as being a jock goes, I grew up a frustrated failure. I had neither the build nor the competitive psyche to become an athlete. Unfortunately in our society, there is a strong connection between being a jock and being a "real man." As a boy becomes a teenager and then an adult, he learns to associate his sexual identity with his physical prowess and with corresponding psychological qualities (competitiveness, aggressiveness, the ability to "take it") that are associated with athletes. For the nonathlete like myself, this can cause serious problems during adolescence. Society has effectively defined him out of his own manhood.

I had a lot of problems with this kind of thing and with my sexual identity while I was growing up as a teenager. I have about as much chance of fitting the traditional role of sexuality in men—physical, aggressive, knowledgeable about such things as cars and women—as I have of hitting a home run in Fenway Park. The problem that I had, however, and I know from discussions with other men that this is actually quite common, is that I really bought the traditional picture of what a man was supposed to be like. After all, my older brother, who was the athletic type and who fit the traditional role in many ways, was really a stud with the women and someone to be looked up to. The result was that I was always trying or wishing to be someone I wasn't, and rejecting these parts of me that were "unmanly." (This trying to be someone other than myself resulted in a traumatic first try with intercourse. When I tried to penetrate the young woman I was with, suddenly my penis got soft. I was horrified. Fortunately, the person I was with was very understanding, and we spent the evening talking about that and other issues and societal pressures we were grappling with. My later attempts at intercourse went fine. Guess it was because I was letting myself be me—instead of someone else.) It wasn't until much later, after college, psychotherapy, and sexual experiences had helped me grow up, that I could begin to fully accept myself as a sexual male. I think this is a fairly common phenomenon—this thing about trying to be something we aren't; you see it in young boys trying to act cool and tough. We all did it because we thought we had to do it in order to make it with women—the ultimate value in adolescent society (and a value that perverts women from friends into sex objects).

I should hasten to add that what I'm really talking about regarding the traditional roles of men is not the physical attributes of the athlete, but the psychological ones. After all, most men can't try to be football players, but most men can try to be competitive, dominant, rational (in a manner that implies nonemotional), aggressive and so on *ad nauseam*. But for many men, living up to these qualities can be rough, both in growing up and in living in adult society. There are a lot of men like me who either don't possess the above manly qualities (and who cause themselves a lot of pain in trying to acquire them) or who, more importantly, did not wish to possess them, because as they grew older they realized that other qualities may be more useful in dealing with other human beings who just happen to be of the opposite sex. (I just wish I could put myself more in the second group than the first.)

But the problem is that the qualities I most like to associate with myself—intelligence, understanding, sensitivity, being emotionally warm and supportive—were not, until the last few years, socially acceptable male values. "Hey, whatsa matter, kid, those are the things that a woman's supposed to act-be-do—not you, you're a man. Ya want people to think you're a fag?" So unless you had an awful lot of courage (I didn't) you grew up subverting your sexuality to other people's whims and not understanding why.

But now, thank God, times are changing. The women's movement has helped a lot in freeing men from these old traditional and stifling roles. I don't know what it's like in adolescent society or in the older generation (though the popularity of NFL football makes me worry), but at least in my age group there're as many men like me as there are like my brother. Some men are learning to be more concerned about their humanity than their manliness, and that's good—for themselves and for society.

I am learning to change, too. Through psychotherapy and with the help of several kind and sensitive friends, both male and female, I have learned to accept and to treasure my own sexuality for what it is. But it has not been easy. I may talk about traditional roles with a sort of intellectual aloofness, but beneath my highfalutin words there lies an awful lot of pain. There are scars from my youth, when I could not understand my own sexuality or why I couldn't be a "real man," that may never heal. Pray to God that they help me teach my own son how to be *human*, not just to be a *man*. I know too that there are still going to be problems, and that the old sexual stereotypes are hard to break. I may have accepted my own kind of male sexuality, on an intellectual level, but on a gut level it's a lot rougher; whenever I'm lonely and my love life is not going well, I find myself wishing that I were the kind of man who could be back in Fenway Park, hitting that home run.

Men in their 20s have many fantasies similar to men in their 30s and 40s. But there are also some differences. Very few men in their 20s have fantasies of sex with a prostitute or "wanton" woman. Their fantasies are usually concerned with relating to the woman they are having sex with, and being desired. They experiment in their fantasies and often incorporate variations of oral and anal sex.

In contrast to older men who have more specific ideas about what traits women find attractive about them—strong arms, their eyes, their penis, etc.—the younger men think more in terms of more diffuse qualities such as a special aura or "vibrations." Their larger view of sexual attractiveness (and this includes the qualities they find attractive in women) is probably due to two main factors. First, the younger men have generally less experience on which to base specific conclusions. Second, they are not as visually and "part" oriented. They tend to consider the total person instead of only breasts or mouth or buttocks. Their sensuality is more holistic than that of the older, traditional male, who learned to be sexually aroused by "things" and body areas, and to stress his visual sense over a more diffused sensuality.

It also appears that the older a man the more likely he is to want his sexual fantasies to come true. While younger men have a great variety of fantasies, they—especially those under 25—don't necessarily choose to carry out many of these thoughts. Part of this may be due to their not having experienced as many sexual diversions as older men and their not having the same immediate need to experience more novel activities. Another explanation for many of these men is that since—like many women—they associate sex with a more holistic sensuality and with relationships, they are not as interested in going forth immediatey to try new techniques and activities. This is not to say that they intend to limit their sexual exploration, but rather that they want to explore with their partners and let new activities "flow"—becoming a part of the exploration in due time. Since their sexuality has not been as repressed and object oriented as that of their predecessors, and perhaps because they are just getting started in sex, these young men don't feel the same desperate urge to compensate for less permissive years. And of course the experienced older men have more fantasies based on experiences they've had and would like to repeat.

The sexual fantasies of the college-educated men in this age group are more romantic and elaborate than those of the less-educated young men and older men of all educational levels. In fact, their fantasies are more similar—in terms of storytelling and holistic concerns—to the fantasies of the women their age and in their educational group than to those of older males.

I think about lying next to a particular girl I once knew and stroking back and forth over her buttocks with the inside of my thigh. I try to imagine as vividly as possible the actual sensation. I also think about her fondling my genitals and my even having an orgasm through contact with her breasts or buttocks alone.

My masturbatory fantasies are always just about fucking, some variations in positions, but nothing bizarre. The main point seems to be to hold out as long as possible to make the girl have an orgasm. I have never been able to give a girl an orgasm through fucking alone, but I would like to.

7

The Golden Years

The man in his fifties has either "made it" by this time or he hasn't. "Making it" usually means succeeding in terms of the American dream—achieving high status in business and the community and successfully raising a family. "Making it" means being able to nonchalantly refer to "my son the doctor." "Making it" means having.

If he's "made it" in these traditional respects, he may be looking around him for other challenges, other mountains to climb. Or he might be sitting on his executive laurels trying to decide how to benefit from and finally enjoy the rewards of his labors. On the other hand, he might be so much a part of the success machinery that he moves almost with the same momentum as in years past and doesn't allow himself time to stop to get in touch with himself or reevaluate the direction of his life. As Snuffy Smith says, "Time's a wasting." And if our man doesn't stop striving perhaps he can trick the clock ticking away the remaining years of his life, or maybe he can somehow sneak by it unnoticed.

If he hasn't "made it" by his group's standards, he might not be concerned. Having a different sense of himself and having decided not to get caught up in "establishment expectations," he set his own goals and directions and now feels a self-fulfillment that his peers don't understand.

Or he may feel tremendous anger at himself and others for his "failure." He might either try desperately to put everything right in an impossibly short time or else induge in self-destruction. He can self-destruct in many ways. The most popular method is alcohol. It's a socially acceptable expression of his "death wish" and numbs any second thoughts.

Whether successful or not in his own or others' terms, he is dealing more directly than he ever has with the inevitability of getting old. He's shocked into a confrontation with his own mortality as he starts attending colleagues' funerals. He has to face death in a society which stays as far away from the subject as possible. In dealing with it he may want desperately to make up for lost time, or he may feel at peace with himself that he has lived a full existence.

The type who "made it" set up a support mechanism in business years ago which gave him an edge over his competitors. He knew how to choose professional allies and to make the most out of female loyalty. Now, in his middle or late 50s, he relies even more upon the latter, but it is a symbiotic mechanism.

He guards his fortress jealously; he has created a sturdy one, often holding a high position in his profession. Demanding maternal wifely compliance from his secretary and secretarial obedience and loyalty from his wife, he ensures that both keep operating the machinery which maintains his power and prestige. He's a wise businessman. He knew long ago it was smarter to nurture a loyal, efficient secretary to keep the business progressing than to have a beautiful assistant. Also in her 50s now, his secretary has been with him for years. Societal traditionalists would unkindly refer to her as a "battle axe." A talented woman with uncommon acuity, she opted for public spinsterhood. By this time she's a bit eccentric in her character, anticipates magnificently, and runs the office with clocklike precision. He has made her all his. Having no family, her loyalties are deeply invested in him and the job. She stays late into the evening to finish the necessary reports and staunchly protects her boss, supporting him in every way.

"Mr. Stability" has found a comfortable equilibrium in his life. He and his wife have a clear partnership—almost a contractual understanding. She will operate the home, and will be paid great deference. He will work long and hard—often an 8:30 A.M.–8:30 P.M. double shift with two secretaries who stagger their stints. The aim of the partnership seems to be to reap the maximum from the most productive period of his busy life. Financial security, education of the children, and decelerated 60s seem to be the goal. They lead a very private social life—maybe a few close friends in for cards, or an occasional jaunt to the cinema or theater.

He conducts business in an excellent fashion—respectable and responsible. If he must attend a convention he goes to his room early in the evening, calling his wife before retiring. He'll often be very effective at work—a senior vice-president perhaps—but with a low profile. He advanced by quiet achievement instead of loudly professed ambition. Almost an isolationist within the organization, he is its Rock of Gibraltar. He's a calm person liked by most colleagues; he doesn't participate in office politics. He's well looked upon by those in the lower echelons; he is in nobody's camp. Organizational upheavals go by him; he remains in place and is usually in favor with the person entrenched at the very top of the corporation. He stays with the same company for many years.

Stable in his sexual and family life as well, he has probably not had an affair. He doesn't look upon sex as paramount and focuses his energies and affections on his family. (Religion may reinforce his "straight and narrow" traits.) He shows great sensuality with his mother and father and the kids. He has spent his fatherly hours socializing with the children and almost consciously buttressing his whole family against outside encroachment. He is at peace with himself. He hasn't asked too many questions about his life but has accepted, sacrificed, given, and worked hard in true Horatio Alger fashion. He hasn't experienced those ecstatic highs or those desperate lows. He knows the satisfactions of the golden mean.

"Last chance Charlie" feels he has to make up for lost time quickly. He has to hustle to make it up the remaining rungs of the success ladder. To exacerbate his panicky struggle, he knows that his company, in which he invested his hopes for future successes and pension benefits, may retire him early and hire a younger, less costly worker in his place. In his last-ditch attempts, he may snatch at any hopeful ally along the way. In trying to cajole his immediate superiors, he is willing to change his former behavior, to adapt to what he thinks they want from him now. He's not above using women around him to get the employment status so important to him. He may even hire a sexy, provocative young woman as his secretary to impress clients and colleagues or to keep his superiors amused and/or impressed. He'll use his wife as well. Suddenly she'll be showering the right people with dinner invitations and attending numerous parties. You can almost see the sweat of panic on his brow as he frantically tries to gather financial security for his impending retirement. He will also grab for the companionship of young women in order to build up his ego and assure himself that the sands in the hourglass aren't running out as fast as they seem to be.

I think I'm in male menopause, with strong tendencies toward satyriasis. I stare at women, want them in bed. Speculate.

Reacting like Charlie to impending old age, the Ponce de Leon type searches frantically for the fountain of youth. Dressed in incongruous attire, he frequents the discotheques and tries to be "cool" like his juniors. He may also hang out with a bawdy crowd of friends his own age, and increase his visits to call girls and street hookers.

More likely, he'll have affairs—semiserious in nature—with women twenty and thirty years his junior. He may even leave his wife of many years, and his several children, to pursue his need for a restorative.

University professors are especially tempted by this. Tenured and bored and surrounded by the youth culture, they are immensely susceptible to their beautiful and intelligent young female students. Quite taken by these women who idolize their position and their wisdom, these academics bask in the attentions and favors of such coeds, while their wives continue for years as if nothing is happening. Her husband, she believes, is going through a phase, and it's her duty to wait patiently and sympathetically for his return.

You know I'm really not happy at home anymore. The children have left the nest and my wife and I have little in common. But somehow I wouldn't feel comfortable going after the students around here who're generally twenty or thirty years younger than I. Sometimes it's awfully tempting—there are some beautiful, intriguing young women on campus. Sometimes when one leaves my office after a conference, I'm almost ready to capitulate. It's amazing. You see so many older professors around here with young women. It's almost the rule these days rather than the exception. Awfully tempting—but not sure I'm ready to play the father role.

A final example—a man in his 50s who feels good about where he's at. He has worked hard, faced life's challenges squarely, and still has a lot of life left in him. He's not so worried about growing old; things just keep getting better for him. His career is more secure than in his younger days and his successes have given him great confidence in himself. Not so threatened by the cultural revolution going on about him, he wants to dabble in the change it has wrought. In many ways this man is ageless. He didn't stop learning or growing. He philosophically looks upon life as a novel and wants to stick around till the final chapter. He's a man of inner strength and outer charm and others are drawn to him. He's also still ready to learn in love and allows himself to care about and yet challenge tradition. But things can get confusing after so many years of marriage, when a vibrant and intelligent "other woman" comes along.

> Wouldn't it be nice to be living with Leslie instead of seeing her now and then. When will I solve the dilemma—married to Barbara, in love with Leslie? Lousy job. Each time with Leslie is different. She is tender, aggressive, and skilled. When we make love it's sensational. When I'm inside her she kegels* the head of my penis and makes me come with more power and release than I've ever experienced. I want to eat her for about three days without stopping. Delicious woman—brain and body.

But between his finesse and fairness, he'll work things out somehow.

Why should the senior male in his 60s be criticized as a "dirty old man" just because he's still a vital and sexual being? Why should sex, like much of American life, be monopolized by the young? Don't experience and wisdom count for much anymore? Many of our senior citizens are still feeling sexy, but it's hard to know what to do about it. Women who are now in their 60s find it almost impossible to break out of the "good

---

* Exercises to help women become more sexually responsive.

girl–bad girl" double standard they were raised by and bound to. They minimize their sexual interests and activities because the opportunities appear so limited.

Elderly men and women are treated by the younger generations as if they shouldn't have sexual interests. They're criticized for any "hanky-panky" and treated like naughty children for alleged sexual indiscretions. Often lonely and frustrated, they encounter many social obstacles as they try to relate across male-female lines. Dating and deep friendships with persons of the opposite sex have not been prominent in their experience. Seniors grew up in a sexually segregated atmosphere where men retired after dinner to smoke cigars while the women did the dishes.

Some of the senior male's best friends have passed on—sobering him as to the inevitable yet making life seem more precious at the same time. Interested in making his final years the best they can be, he is often more occupied with issues other than sex. Yet sex is a part of his life and demands some thought and attention. Sexual desire is not as great as before, but it's certainly there. Besides, he must prove himself still potent in many ways, and sex is a major means for doing so. Retirement is supposed to happen in this decade of life, and our man in his 60s has either planned financial security and retirement or is protesting the inevitable.

I may not be as interested in sex as I was as a younger man. But let me tell you the interest is still there. I can still admire a pretty girl like the rest of them. Maybe I can't get up for things as much as in the past, but there are other things that are important like caressing, oral sex, just plain having fun in many ways.

•

I've been alone for almost three years since my wife died. I'd like to have a companion and a woman to enjoy being with. But either the women I meet are a bunch of vultures, just looking desperately for someone with pants on, or they're young and pretty but not interested in me.

•

During copulation, I like the use of a good-size mirror to show how the penis glides in and out of the vagina or anus. This can show if the vagina has tumefied sufficiently to get good action without buckling the penis. The mirror should also have a slight magnification, especially to show the penis enlarged. This will stimulate the ego and in this way give additional pleasure.

•

Married my secretary a few years ago and that girl is trying to kill me. I like sex all right, but I'm not as young as I used to be.

•

My wife keeps pestering me for sex. I finally said, "Molly, aren't you getting too old for that kind of thing?"

One gentleman summed it up nicely: "I had a prostate operation eight months ago. It slowed me down for a while and was an honest-to-God scare, but now I'm back at having sex, at least once a week. It's still a fine part of life to savor. Hell, Picasso was still going strong at 90. Who says ya got to stop at retirement age. You're as old as you feel and as old as you do."

8

The Tumescent Teens

They're learning about themselves and sex. They're looking for models, reading books, exploring. Barraged by explicit reminders of sex all around them, they often feel pressured to try sex early. To be a virgin at 20 is considered an oddity.

The young men who decided not to go to college are following the more traditional sexual routes while most college students are coping with the more assertive and sexually experimenting female. Such turning of the sexual tables has its problems. Some of the young men, put off by being the objects of sexual pursuit, are retreating.

"Getting together" is replacing the more formal dating routine. Teens spend time together in groups or in pairs as friends and lovers. Young men and women see themselves as individuals first, potential wives and husbands second. They break out of traditional sex roles more easily than their elders, and their sexual fantasies are more diffuse. They have relatively limited experience to draw on for specifics, yet they dream and romanticize and feel sexually aroused much of the time.

What's embarrassing is when you're dancing a slow dance and you get hard and the girl can feel it.

•

Some days I feel horny all day and don't know what to do with it. I've made love a few times, but it's important to me to really like the girl I'm with. Maybe when I go off to school I'll meet someone and we can live together.

•

I daydream about seeing a good-looking girl on the beach, pool, or street and walk up and kiss them and say hi. We may go out and have a good time, see a show or dance, and go back to my place and have a warm time together making love.

•

I'll tell you sometimes I try my best not to think about sex so I won't get a hard-on. I get hard so easily, and it can be real embarrassing. Like when I was in class the other day thinking about feeling and screwing the girl across from me. Then the bell rang. Here I am sitting, afraid to get up 'cause I've got this gigantic hard-on and it wouldn't go away. You know girls can tell things like that. So I tried to be cool and cover it with my notebook. Just made me realize I have to plan better and not get turned on at times like that.

The content of fantasy is affected of course by experiences the person has had. Teenagers who have not yet experienced intercourse may fantasize occasionally what it would be like, but their sexual thoughts are more apt to center around kissing, fondling, and foreplay, with a great many romantic overtones or concerns with the logistics of carrying out a specific and special sexual activity not yet tried.

I'm 14 years old and have never made it with a girl —would like to but will wait until the "right time." In fact, I'm a bit scared. I don't know if I'll do it the right way, but I guess practice makes perfect. Like you know when I first started kissing girls—when I was about 12—I wasn't sure exactly how. I thought it'd be so easy, but then I tried once and our noses got in the way. Noses. Now I didn't think much about noses when I was a kid and dreamed of kissing or saw all that kissing on TV or at the show. So then I watched a little closer to see how the people turned a little to kiss and didn't bump noses. I still don't know exactly how wet a kiss is supposed to be or when to put my tongue in. I have a lot of thoughts about that. Right now I'm learning about bras and how to be cool about undoing one. Wow. It's not easy. Some snap in the back—some in the front. You know you don't like to look like you're checking a chick's bra out, but I just want to get an idea. Don't know if I should let her undo her own bra—women's lib you know—or if she's always wearing one. I guess every guy learns that stuff. I just get nervous. Maybe I should practice on girls I'm not really into until I can do it right.

•

I'm sixteen. I've had sex a couple of times—was usually high. And hey man it was great. Great chicks —great feeling. I read magazines that tell about having the girl put her mouth on you or eating her out. I think I'd like her to do that to me—don't know how to ask, but don't know if I'd really like putting my mouth on her.

In contrast with many men 35 and over who had their first intercourse with a prostitute, as a "gang bang" participant, or sometimes with a girlfriend in the back seat of a car or in secret elsewhere, today's teenagers are freer and more natural in their sexual encounters. They tend to have their first experience with a friend of the opposite sex or a young woman with whom they are emotionally involved. It is not unheard of for some liberated parents to allow their teenage son or daughter to spend the night at home in the company of a person with whom they are infatuated. Teenage parties are less supervised than they used to be, and permissive dorm regulations, beach gatherings, camping trips, and certainly the popularity of vans all present opportunities for less illicit, and less clandestine, sex than in the past. (It would, in fact, be interesting to survey these same teenagers in about twenty years to see if clandestine sexual fantasies are as popular among them as they are now among men over 35.)

Here are some examples of first times:

I'd gone down to visit my cousin in San Diego for the summer. She had a dynamite friend and we got along at once. Terry, the friend, was 17, a year older than me at the time. She was fine. Long blond hair and breasts that were really big. It was hard to keep my hands off of her. I was hard much of the time. After about three weeks—and I saw Terry much of that time—she told me her parents were going to Mexico for the three-day weekend. So I went to stay with her. Now she'd had sex before so she knew what to do. That first night we made love all night. I'm not kidding you. I was so sore the next day I couldn't believe it. But you know the first time I tried to get in her I was so excited and I guess nervous that I shot off before I really got inside. Ain't that a bitch. But she didn't seem upset and within a few minutes I was hard again. I'll tell you she was one beautiful woman. We still write each other, and she visits me at college sometimes. She's great! I couldn't have asked for a better introduction.

•

I was only 13. The girl next door and I were messing around one day, and her mother had gone to the store. I was feeling all over the girl and asked her to show me her breasts and how big they'd gotten. She started to unbutton her blouse, then I got real hard. She could see that. Then I put my hand in her pants, and we decided to hurry up and go to the bedroom. We had sex on her bed with still much of our clothes on 'cause we were afraid her mom would come home and catch us. I came almost right away. We wanted to try again, but were afraid. So we got dressed and got out of the house so nobody would be suspicious.

•

Jackie and I were both 16 and had been going together for two years. Her parents had told her that if we were going to have sex it would be all right in her room. They wanted us to sort of plan for it so we had contraception and everything. Jackie lives in a big three-story house and her room is really private. So we went back to Jackie's and made love. It was one of the most beautiful experiences I've had.

•

Hey, I met this far-out chick at a party. We were dancing real close and she was pushing and rubbing against my dick—made me real hard. So I said, "You don't mess around like that, baby, unless you mean business." We went out in the backyard when the music got fast, and then we fucked. I was 11 then.

•

I got real high at this party. Then some kids were going to some of the back rooms. I went in and saw some of them making love. They were really fucked up too. So I joined in. The girl I was with—I don't think she cared who was in her, she was just really grooving. Came three or four times with her. Then we collapsed. I slept for a while, then got dressed and left.

•

A bunch of us were at the beach. One of the girls—who I always thought really liked me—and I went swimming together. We swam for a while, then we were just playing and talking out in the waves. I kissed her and we both got really turned on. It just happened so fast. I had my hands in her bathing suit—feeling her breasts and her vagina. She was all wet and slippery. It was starting to get dark and I suggested we go off near one of the caves—away from everyone. She said O.K. and we went and made love.

●

I was 10 and had this beautiful baby sitter. One night when my parents were going to be out really late, I went and took a bath and got in my pajamas. The baby sitter walked in just before I got the bottoms completely on. She came over and we were sort of laughing. God, I was embarrassed, but I'd had fantasies about feeling her for years. She started to sort of touch my penis and it was hard as can be. I started rubbing her big breasts like I'd wanted to do so long. She slowly undressed me, then took off her clothes. I was amazed at her two big breasts and a little scared at all the hair below to see her naked. She laid on the bed and had me get on top of her. I came all over her before I got in. But when I got hard again she guided me in. It was over soon again, but I didn't know the difference. After that night, she and I used to fuck as often as we could, till she went off to college about six months later. I really really missed her.

Although sex may generally be easier, teenagers today have more pressure on them to have sex early. These are unsure years for most. Experiencing both physical and social changes, they often feel awkward, left out, or just plain don't know what to do. They feel their own sexual energy, and there is considerable peer pressure to do something about it. What is really important to most teenagers is being accepted by the others. They are breaking away and trying to be independent from parents while at the same time looking for praise and understanding from teachers and friends. It's not easy, especially when church, school, and family say one thing, and the liberated say another.

Some teenagers, feeling pressures to be sexual and nonchalant, but afraid they won't be accepted, go through traumatic times.

Most of the guys my age have made love. I haven't. Guess I'm just not a handsome dude. The girls don't fall over me. Some days I get so embarrassed—like when my face breaks out real bad—I really don't want to go out of my home. I just never seem to know how to talk to a girl—always feel so silly—like what should I say?

•

I'm shorter than most of the girls. It's awful. Mom says I'll grow—that the girls just get tall faster then stop growing. She says I'll start passing them about ninth or tenth grade. So what do I do now? I really like Erica—this girl in my English class—but don't think she even notices me. She's taller than me.

•

Most of the guys in my dorm get together with the chicks, and some are living together. I just sit in my room and try to study a lot of the time. I wonder if there will ever be a girl who'll love me.

The trials of puberty remain. However, never before has the so-called younger generation been subjected to such conflicting instructions or been faced with such differing expectations.

9

Other

By sheer weight of numbers, the typical American male is middle class, white, and heterosexual. Men of other races, classes, and sexual persuasions may play major roles in the society and in the shaping of its attitudes, but have been greatly ignored in terms of their individual situations.

The Black male athlete, for instance, may be lauded on the field of athletic battle and venerated as a star, as the best in a very manly undertaking. However, the Black male's sexual attitudes and experiences are rarely explored. They are "sensitive" subjects that popular magazines and other media are loath to examine and even pointedly ignore. Likewise, researchers (Kinsey among them) regularly exclude Blacks from their studies on the grounds that not enough of a sampling could be obtained. And it is true—timidity about including Blacks in psychological studies has resulted in a scarcity of basic research information. This has been compounded by the Black community's understandable distrust and unwillingness to co-operate with white empiricists attempting to delve into their private lives.

This has been less true of male homosexuals in this country, but not by much. Ironically, they too may often be publicly applauded as stars of key cultural, image-forming fields such as movies, theater, television, fashion, and sports. However, the nature of their sexuality has largely remained in the closet of the national consciousness until very recently.

Given the past neglect of such groups, it is impossible for anything but a glancing attempt to be made as far as examining such groups. But the attempt must be made so as to begin the groundwork, no matter how insufficient. Obviously the Black man and the male homosexual do not belong in the juxtaposition in which I have placed them, except by virtue of neglect. Let me point out, however, that both also play major though ill-defined roles in the sexual psyche of the white, heterosexual American male.

Very little has been written in this country about Black men and their sexuality. Much of this has remained a dark secret—to the white world especially—and consequently fostered legends, myths, and misunderstandings.

Skin color does not automatically create a new type of sexuality. In fact, many of the differences in sexual behavior, attitudes, and fantasies among Black men of varying socioeconomic and education groups are similar to the differences Kinsey found among white men in the 1940s.* Furthermore, a middle- or upper-class Black man is more like his white counterpart in his sexuality than like his lower-income Black "brother."

Skin color does, however, make a difference because

---

* The cultural gaps between white males are not as significant as they were in Kinsey's time. Lower-income white males are more middle class these days in their sexuality than they were. This is probably due to influences of the media as well as to the changing roles of women regarding their sexuality.

we in America have decided it does. Born with dark skin, a male is born into certain racial orientations and societal limitations, and these cannot be minimized. A Black boy hears stories from other Blacks about what he is supposed to be like sexually and what white boys are supposedly like.

You know, when I was growing up in the ghetto, I used to think that it was a terrible thing to "eat pussy." I heard the white boys did it and it sounded disgusting. Older and wiser now, I enjoy going down on a woman I care for—it's actually very enjoyable, and I feel there are many ways to add to a partner's pleasure besides banging away inside her.

He learns that it is not popular to show interest in white girls. But while growing up in the 1940s–50s, that's about all he saw in magazines and movies and on television.

While the white boys were in neighborhoods hearing stories about the alleged enormity of the typical Black man's penis, the Black boys were hearing stories also about how big their penises were supposed to be. They also heard that playing with the penis and masturbating would make it grow bigger.

When we masturbated as kids we primarily did it— no I can't say it was a fad—rather a mischievous thing to do. We did it to see who could come the fastest with sort of a belief that the more you play with yourself the bigger your dick grows to be. That was the main reason we masturbated. But also I think it's a natural instinct for men (both Black and white) to do. Maybe more if you're Black you tend to hold or play with your penis—sort of publicly. In the ghetto, you see guys going down the street doing this (I never saw white guys doing that), or put your hands in your pocket and play, or even put holes in your pocket and play with it. We were aware that girls look at penises so we walked down the street with our hands in our pockets holding our penises real tight in hopes it would arouse someone.

•

We called it a "handmade dick"—believing that a boy could increase his penis size by playing with it and/or masturbating.

In comparison with their white middle-class counterparts, these young men from ghetto and poor rural areas had sexual relations with girls and women at a much earlier age. Their first experience with intercourse might have been even before their early teens.

I grew up in the country outside Jackson, Mississippi —didn't hear directly that much about sex, but we knew at a very young age what happened between men and women. I can remember when I was about 4 or 5 I used to wait until the adults were at dinner, then two of my girl cousins and I went underneath the porch, and I used to put my dick inside each one of them and go up and down like we were having sex. Not a whole lot could happen at that age, but the feeling was good and I know the girls enjoyed it, too.

•

My first real intercourse was when I was 14. I was walking my girlfriend home from a dance, and we slipped into a dark alley and had sex standing up.

As their sexual relations increased, they felt that masturbation should be secondary to the "real thing." They were told stories about what manhood meant— fulfilling a woman sexually with your penis—and consequently they didn't spend much time or energy in foreplay. They heard that white men participated in oral sex, especially cunnilingus. And they reacted against this, thinking it a dirty thing to do or unnecessary for anyone who had adequate apparatus. As one young man said, "If my dick isn't good enough for her, I

148

don't want her." Other differences were evident, too, in their upbringing.

> You know I'm from the ol' South. What is interesting to me is that the white boys talk about their "cock" (meaning their penis). The first time I heard that I couldn't believe it 'cause when I was growin' up cock was what the woman has. I don't know if this is mostly southern or Black, but I sure know that men didn't have cocks. I remember a poem we used to say as kids. "Two lil' boys sittin' on a rock, lookin', lookin', at Sally's cock."

Besides concern about having a large enough penis, Black men—especially in the lower-income groups—felt social pressures regarding their sexuality. They had to prove their manhood by dominating and sexually fulfilling women. For some this was the only means available for accomplishment; for feeling successful.* Uneducated, untrained, and discriminated against, few made it up that white ladder of success. There are not many ways to feel like a man in America when you're unemployed. And so sexual prowess took on a special significance. Also, without money one finds few affordable diversions and enjoyments available beyond sex.

Most Black men who have "made it" in the white world are a part of the unique social transition group which has upped its social status in one generation. Raised in relatively poor households segregated from the white community, they now mingle and compete in the white world. These forerunners of "social transitions"† have assimilated the sexual training from childhood and from their new social surroundings into a newly integrated sexuality.

> I only make love to women that really turn me on, that is the only way that I can enjoy the relationship.

---

* Similar to white men of this same socioeconomic category.
† Like the "new woman" or the "liberated" male.

I put her and myself in a very romantic situation—get in the tub and feel each other or think of being at the beach or taking a skinny dip and make love on the floor or in the tub or shower. When she is sleeping, I slowly arouse her and we love again. There must not be any hang-ups, but I am not an exhibitionist.

We all have varying amounts of male and female hormones in our bodies and individual mixes of sexual preference and behavior. Homosexuality, like the rest of human behavior, is not an exclusive, static state. Within the male homosexual community we find everything from those who indulge in exaggerated effeminate behavior and dress—the "queens" who decorate themselves with cosmetics and fine lace and silks—to the "butch" whose behavior rivals and often surpasses our concept of a "man's man." However, liking to dress in women's clothing does not necessarily mean a man indulges in homosexual activity. Many transvestites consider themselves heterosexual in every other way except appearance.

Because of the various degrees of heterosexual and homosexual thoughts and behavior all of us incorporate, there have been heated debates about what constitutes hetero- or homosexual orientation. More than anything, these debates illustrate our great discomfort with homosexuality, especially male homosexuality. The taboos are great. Most American men are deeply fearful of their homosexual tendencies and deny, compensate for, or mask them in many ways. Irrational outrage against male homosexuals is one method. Degrading homosexual jokes serve the same end. Men's fantasies of their wives making love to another man may likewise mask the desire for an encounter with another male. Group sex or orgies provide another opportunity to indirectly act out subconscious homosexual desires, as do sports. Sports bring men together in emotional and physical ways not otherwise condoned. Where else can the male pat his comrade on the fanny, as he does on the basketball court, or in how many other places is he allowed to embrace his fellow male with emotion and sincerity as he can after a hard-fought, grueling football game? (Interestingly, traditional woman-degrading locker-room talk is filled with elements of homosexual camaraderie.)

We are, however, slowly learning to accept the natural homosexual parts of ourselves. Younger people especially are more willing to live with more liberal definitions of masculine-feminine behavior and roles. They seem to have realized that a homosexual fantasy or desire does not constitute a decision to be gay or accept a homosexual orientation. For instance, most women in our society are attracted in some ways to the female body (often more than to the nude male body, in fact) because that's the way they were raised. Growing up in a society which extols the female body, especially breasts and genitals, as a sexual stimulus has resulted in women also becoming aroused by such stimuli.

Since we are educated to our turn-ons by our environment and our experiences, a woman only diverts her sexual attraction to women's bodies when she learns from media or by experience to substitute males as a source of arousal. Most women don't feel uncomfortable being sexually attracted to both men and women. Yet, generally, they will choose only sexual contact with men. But they can naturally, and with societal approval, show love and affection to other women, hugging one another and kissing with ease. American men can't.

People choose homosexuality for a vast number of reasons, emotional as well as physical. Most homosexuals and bisexuals say they are sexually satisfied. The ones who are dissatisfied say there is an emotional void; they would like to love someone and be close—the same desires expressed by heterosexual men.

There are many ways of becoming and being gay. The excerpts from the interview with Eric, which follows, give us some insight into the journey of one of these men.

Eric is a tall, handsome, blond, 30-year-old business-man living in the northeast section of the United States. He was raised a Catholic, but no longer attends church. Divorced after five years of marriage, he and his wife are still good friends and mutually raise their son. Not long after Eric "came out of the closet," his wife became heavily involved with another woman. This to Eric was ironic and somewhat of a relief as he felt he could share his gayness more directly with his former wife.

Eric finds that books and movies influence his sex life only peripherally. Aroused by some pictures and articles in magazines such as the *All Men Catalogue* and *Playgirl,* he doesn't care much for pornographic movies because, as a "video freak," he usually prefers movies with "artistic teasing and beautiful sensuality." Although he occasionally has affairs with women, Eric considers himself "gay." Presently he is not emotionally satisfied with his sex life. He explains:

> I'm very picky. There aren't that many men that are that hot in bed. A lot of the time I enjoy superficial sex, but I find myself in quest of a singular, emotionally fulfilling relationship.
>
> I always knew I was interested in men, but I denied it so much. I was raised Catholic and of course sexuality is very denied in the church, but gayness wasn't even to be considered. I suppose I sublimated it. For example, I was a fanatic for order (perhaps denial or misplaced sex energy). I had to have everything in place and felt uncomfortable if a book was out of place on a library shelf or an ashtray had some ashes in it. (I'm glad to say I can relax more and am not such a compulsively clean and orderly person now.)
>
> Also, ever since I can remember I had a vivid anal curiosity. I discovered it was pleasurable to insert

and move a bobby pin in my rectum. It felt so good. I would try other objects as I got older, and would massage and penetrate my rectum with these other things.

I dated a fair amount in high school and college, but just never got overly excited about the whole routine. It was as if some important element were missing. I did look around and find men around me, but I couldn't handle more than a flashing fantasy about sex with any of them. I sort of thought that one day I might like to try sex with a man, but was not overly concerned about pursuing this, and in fact was quite nervous about the prospect.

One of my first gay experiences was with Jim. I fell head over heels in love. More in love than I have ever been. In fact, although Jim and I have been apart for more than a year and a half, I am still very much in love and haunted by him.

As much as I love Jim, the whole relationship has been a very painful one. He first went back to New England to live with his mother, attempted suicide, and recently went to northern California. I've been thinking a lot about my relationship with him and life in general. I think a lot of things we do are based on power. If a person has a lot of power, they can be held in awe. I think as I grew up, people (male and female) gave me a lot of power because they considered me to be very attractive. For a long time I didn't know how to handle that power, and I probably abused it—and was insensitive to those people. Now that I'm 30, it's okay. Besides, I think one of the reasons I loved Jim so much was that we indulged in a big power play—physically and emotionally. I appreciated that he challenged my power; but I think the reason he left me was that he couldn't deal with giving up some of his power to someone—as he was to me, and I was willing to do to him. Maybe being intimate and in love is exactly that, and he thought he might be annihilated.

Jim used to be dominant in the relationship, but I changed it. So we took turns being dominant and submissive. We would have competition based around strength—wrestling—one against the other—an admiration of each other's and our own body strength. He would get on a real power trip at times and want to make somebody grovel. Jim taught me a whole sense of competition. I loved it, and we shared crazy, beautiful moments together. But I still think he left me 'cause he felt I was taking some of his power. If he could only realize that that's not what I ultimately wanted. There were times when we would have a fight and have sex, and it got scary for me because Jim didn't know how to quit. He had a streak of sadism. I think in this competition and in the power struggle, he saw me as his father, and later when he went to New England—the father/lover struggle drove him to attempt suicide. It's all so complicated. Many of my sexual fantasies—especially my masturbatory ones—are based on Jim.

I think back over the time Jim and I were walking through the woods. He had a beautiful scarf around his neck. We stopped walking. As I stood back to look at him, he unzipped his zipper and let his cock hang out. Once when I was taking a bath, Jim came in and put his leg on the bathtub and pointed his erect cock at me. Very exciting. I think about the beautiful time that I fucked him on a beach on a moonlit night.

In art class a number of years ago we had to do a project which was concentrated on the juxtaposition of unsimilar objects—the model was a razor blade embedded in a baby-bottle nipple. This really fascinated me and gave me crazy funny feelings—which I can't really understand. Somehow I could imagine the bleeding, the cutting that this meant—maybe something about oral vulnerability. Sometimes in masturbating I think about cutting—slicing. One fantasy that comes to mind is that I am fucking Jim and cutting his intestines with my cock.

Another fantasy I have about Jim is a car fantasy. While he was driving I'd sometimes get down on him, and we'd find an exit road and fuck.

I sometimes masturbate with erotic pictures I have that were taken at a park. A guy was standing hitch-hiking and as a car of men came by he took out his huge erect cock out of his pants and waved it—"Come and pick me up."

Other fantasies that appeal to me concern sex in natural environments—even sometimes in sort of stilted nature or intensely made-up romantic places, such as you would see on Hallmark cards. Or I'm standing masturbating above a group of people and they have their mouths open to catch the come. Another time I'm lying in the middle of a gang-bang circle jerk and they're all spurting on me.

My sex is usually with my own age group, probably for the emotional satisfaction it can offer. Older men bother me a little because they tend to be graspy. They aren't so much loving as they are desperate. They also probably make me nervous because they force me to face my own age and the reality that I too am getting older.

One older man with whom I had an enjoyable sex encounter used a wooden rod on me anally.

Sometimes I enjoy sex in a group. I've been to a number of orgies. I suppose I enjoy the voyeuristic part of group sex the most. It turns me on to think of another guy masturbating or watching others having sex. There's almost a comforting feeling that I can watch and don't have to participate.

I enjoy fellatio, but to me it is an isolated—lone—sexual experience. It's more organ, more genitally centered than an awareness of a feeling for the person attached. This is especially true if one person goes down. If both go down on each other it can be more mutually satisfying. But this doesn't happen so often. If two men do this for each other's enjoyment instead of their own, then you can get a feeling of sharing a lot.

I'm attracted to the white male stereotype—a man with light sandy hair, tall, etc. I don't find too many dark men erotic—this has been consistent most of my life. There was a Black guy I found erotic, but it was disturbing because he wanted to leave his lover for me.

I like to think about or have sex in forbidden places—in a rest room, tearoom, some secret corner, movie, etc. It's more exciting when you have a feeling you are doing something you're not supposed to do.

I find myself becoming more and more open to kinky sex—like with animals, sadomasochistic, with devices, etc. In *Giles Goatboy*, these men have become so kinky that normal sex is kinky. I think I would open up more quickly to new things if the climate were right. Like these two friends from San Francisco both fucked me at once.

When I'm fucking, I rarely have an orgasm. Unless I'm really emotionally involved, I don't come.

Men who consider themselves gay sometimes have sex with women. Eric said he had had a brief affair again with a woman a few months earlier, but it was so dissatisfying that he doesn't know if he'll want to have sex with another woman.

In their fantasies about men, a number of women think of faceless, unrecognizable men. Most heterosexual men, in contrast, have their sexual fantasies about women they know or at least have seen before somewhere—no faceless women for them. The gay men who have occasional fantasies about women usually don't have personal knowledge of who these women are:

My fantasies during sexual relations are more often related to men I actually know. Some types of fantasies—such as male-female oral and genital, male-male oral and anal—the woman is usually fictional or someone I don't know but have seen somewhere. She is usually tall and blond and beautiful or a French woman. I have acted out these fantasies several times with other men, but once with a woman.

Many gay men report masturbatory fantasies like Eric's in which they are surrounded by a group of masturbating men who ejaculate on their nude bodies. There is a fascination for the whole male masturbation process and almost a group ritual arousal that is attained by receiving the members' collective sperm. A 35-year-old professor in central Arkansas writes:

During the day while masturbating or even while having sexual relations with someone who is not so interesting, I get very excited by this fantasy. I am in an empty room in the midst of a group of nude men—all extremely virile. I am either on the floor or on a raised platform on my back. Sometimes I am restrained in a "spread-eagle position." At others I assume this position. There are perhaps eight to ten men present—both Black and white. All are surrounding me standing and masturbating. They each in turn ejaculate on my body—usually on the chest and groin—occasionally on the face. I find this extremely exciting and writhe about and eventually climax myself without manipulating myself in any way. Being covered with sperm is enough to cause me to have an orgasm.

Note: I think it's curious that I am never on a bed —seems that is reserved for more intimate sex (one or two males). I've experienced this fantasy with one or two partners, but never as many as the actual fantasy. If given the opportunity, I'd love to do it in a second.

10

Fear, Fun, Pain, and Bondage

A basic fear we all have is that of being rejected, of being left alone. Most other fears and concerns emanate from this. As children we first experience this terrifying feeling of being rejected by those we are closest to and even dependent upon for actual survival.

No doubt the first great separation trauma was expulsion from the womb. This ever-continuing pervasive fear is often generalized in adult years by what is termed "separation anxiety," anxiety being different from fear in that the object of our fear is not known. But a tense, empty, scared feeling persists even though we don't know why.

Adolescent and adult males usually have to confront more actively than do women the possibility of being rejected. The traditional male has to risk rejection every time he asks for a date, every time he makes a sexual advance. Either to confuse issues or to buffer the pain of rejection the traditional woman was supposed to "play hard to get," to say "no" to any and all overtures whether she meant no or not. At the same time, women often didn't know what the man really intended either—if he was approaching her with real interest or fulfilling society's expectations that he make the manly effort. Men have a variety of ways of dealing with the rejection they are told they must frequently risk.

The other complementary and equally terrifying fear is that of being incomplete, of losing one's identity to a dominant, destructive force. Most men are strung between these extremes—rejection on some basis and/or being possessed. These are constant themes in their articulated fears. For example, most men unrealistically fear inadequate penis size. Growing up, they have been led to believe that a large penis is a key to sexual success and being loved—the security against being rejected. Rarely did they know what the "right" size was, but their anxiety increased as they heard stories on the street or furtively glanced at other males' flaccid penises.

Several factors have probably accentuated the anxiety experienced. Little scientific evidence was available, and most women didn't give their real views on the subject. Also, a flaccid penis gives little indication as to the size or shape of an erect penis since it may double in size when erect or may actually increase by five times. Bizarre stories exist about the size of a Black man's penis—because most were seen by "strangers," especially "white strangers," in a flaccid state.

Another fear prevalent now is not being able to fulfill the female sexually—not surprising in an achievement-oriented society. This is often expressed as "giving" her orgasms, preferably one after another, until she collapses in exhaustion. Although common, it has remained in the background in most cultures. In the traditional American society, and most others, men concentrated more on publicly impressing other males with their alleged sexual abilities—hence, the "locker-room syndrome." A great deal of talk went on but not an equal amount of activity. The talk was rarely truthful, but rather an ego-saving and/or promoting game usually destructive and alienating for the female being degraded in absentia.

With the advent of Masters and Johnson and the subsequent study of women and their sexuality, women confirmed and affirmed their sexual fantasies and urges. Unfortunately, this new "truth" was quickly adapted and converted into a new male fear—the fear of not performing accurately or adequately. If a man doesn't "make" his partner have multi-orgasms, he is inadequate. Conversely, if a woman is not capable of multiple orgasms or of having one big, good one, she may be held inadequate.

Impotence happens to *all* men at one time or another, regardless of the logical cause—physical disability, long abstinence, etc.

I had a failure recently. I'd been trying to get it from this one woman for over two years. First she was married, then got divorced and moved into town. When we finally got in bed there was something about her that turned me off—'cause my head's attached to my johnson. She's a beautiful chick with a great body. But there was something wrong. I just couldn't get it up. It really upset me and upset her something fierce. She was already questioning her abilities about some things, relationships, career, etc. So this really got to her. I think one of the things that was working against me and keeping me from functioning was that I thought she might be an emotional burden on me. I was afraid that the demands would be more than I was ready to pay, given my set of circumstances.

So anyhow, this happened twice. We went to bed together, and I couldn't get an erection. Strange, 'cause like I say, I really wanted her. I would get hard when she was playing with me—but then I'd try to stick it in and the thing goes "droop." (This not being able to get it up happens to me sometimes when it's the first time with a woman—the anxiety and all that. If a woman doesn't understand me or that it happens at times to all men, then it could be even more devastating.) She claimed to have this thing about me. There were a number of men interested in her, but she wasn't sleeping with any of them. Seems that she just wanted to be with me. Finally, the second time I couldn't get it up, she said, "You have to help me." What she wanted me to do was help her masturbate. I manipulated her boobs and played with her johnson while she masturbated herself. It was an interesting experience.

I'm really afraid to try sex with her again, 'cause the failure to get it up affects my own ego, my own actual abilities, and other relationships.

•

When I can't function well sexually it's usually because I really don't want to be in the situation but feel obliged to be. Or I have to be somewhere, like it's two or three in the morning and I know I should be home. I might be thinking about the drive home. I have to feel secure in a sexual situation. I guess I'm really vulnerable while making love and want to be able to concentrate and not be disturbed.

Second only to impotence is the fear of coming too soon. Embarrassing, humiliating, but normal. Now finally aware of women's interest in sexual enjoyment, the male may consider it important to resist orgasm as long as possible, even if that means thinking about the unsexiest subject imaginable in order to accomplish this end.

And there is the often-related fear of aging, of losing physical ability. It is feared by most, especially when told that the male's "sexual prime" occurs at 18 or 19 years of age and a woman's at 35. This is coupled with a fear of losing one's physical attractiveness with age, especially within a society where youth is venerated and the elderly are shunted aside. To compensate for the loss of his youth and accompanying prowess, the male strives for success in business and praise for consequent status. (Ironically, this very compensation often takes so much time and energy that one may age even more rapidly.)

Humor is an essential health mechanism. Through it we release tensions. Study the humor and ironies of any group and you will know what it considers important, what it dreads, and what it resents. You will also know what issues it doesn't want to bring to the surface, as well as what it enjoys. In humor we can vie indirectly with others and laugh at them as well as with them at ourselves. Sex jokes are popular among the older age groups.

Overheard in impressive law offices, at afternoon cocktail parties, in locker rooms, or on construction sites, very often the jokes center around sexual subjects of particular concern and uneasiness to white males—Blacks, broads, and brotherly love.

Attributing stupendous sexual prowess to the Black man, Black jokes often focus on his allegedly enormous penis and base animalistic abilities. It is as if the tellers of these stories paradoxically combine their fear of and fascination with the Black lover. They want to be like their image of the Black stud, but resist him for his perceived talents. They gape at the Black lover in their stag shows and get turned on in an intense and secret way.

And as much as they fear this perceived Black challenge to their women, they are obsessed by and indirectly encourage it. For instance, it's not uncommon for a white male to use, as a seductive tactic, a joke about the Black man's big genitals. He hopes to turn on his glistening white prey and in turn enjoy the illusion he is creating. Or he might use the joke as a ploy to find out her sexual interests. Yet in the presence of a woman who he knows had dated men of another race, he may exhibit vague disgust. But he will always want to ask the question what was it like?

Darkness often represents to such men the clandestine dirtiness of sex. Black women are supposed to be wild, wanton lovers who can be bought, sequestered, and ravished in hidden places. In some quarters, superstitions have been converted into half-serious jokes. Men in their 40s, for instance, say that in certain northeastern cities it was held that if you had sex with a Black woman your luck would change for the better.

In their jokes women are presented in a degrading fashion, supporting Freud's supposition in the Victorian era that, because of societal pressures to abstain from sex for so long in their youth, men had to debase their sexual object in order to find enjoyment. Popular among those brought up to feel that sex is dirty and surreptitious are base comments ranging from the poundage of a female's breast to the slant of her vagina. Nymphomaniacs are especially common ribald subjects.*

Much of this humor emanates from fears of being surpassed by the Black man, dangerously engulfed by the female, and being raped and left powerless. Comments and jokes about male homosexuality are more repressed and uncertain and nearly always cruel because many men are fearful of any sort of homosexual association. Their anxiety and repulsion render unrecognizable any natural homosexual feelings they may possess. Younger men may more easily indulge in some sexual encounters with other men, or at least fantasize the possibilities. The closest the older male comes to this is in oblique sexual bouts with other men—usually with a safe psychological screen. For example, the popular fantasy of their wives having intercourse with

---

* There are sexually promiscuous and psychologically unfulfilled women just as there are such men (the male Don Juan stereotype). Nymphomania, however, is a misused sexual term, a remnant from the Victorian era, when a woman with sexual desire was considered a misfit.

other men allows them to visualize men nude and in action while remaining shielded from a direct homosexual threat. Their fascination with and enjoyment of oral sex can also include homosexual overtones.

Obsessive concerns of a number of these men are concentrated upon the perceived sexuality of Black men and women, lusty and "inferior" white women, and "corrupt" homosexuals. Raised in a puritanical framework which mythologized or closeted these individuals, many men base much of their in-group humor and locker-room discussions on these sexually suspect outsiders.

Power and achievement—it's male, and it's American, though no longer exclusively so. In a society where mobility is possible, where we are told that our status depends on our accomplishments, we "make it" by our achievements, our actions, and we look about for praise for our performance. We prove our worth constantly by doing. So we *do*. It's an exciting and responsible situation in which to be. We can't say "This is the social level at which I was born and at which I'll stay."

As more opportunities arise, however, so do the number of heart attacks, ulcers, and other by-products of "striving" stress. The male, like any human being, wants love, warmth, and affection, but must himself be tough and unyielding, and not succumb to "petty" emotions or fears, whether in business or in bed. The warrior was born with a penis to wield and must succeed in conquering the woman in order to prove his worth. It is no surprise, therefore, that so many men have sexual fantasies concerned with power and achievement. These fantasies cover a broad spectrum, including the most cogent expression of personal power—forceful domination of his sexual partner.

Why do some people choose to combine pain with sexuality? What type of turn-ons, if any, do they derive from this, and how do their activities relate to their upbringing and personality?

Sadomasochism is the term which describes the incorporation of some degree of pain in sexual behavior. A sadist is a person who enjoys inflicting pain on another, and a masochist derives enjoyment, or at least some reinforcement, from being the sufferer, the victim, and having pain inflicted. All of us have some sadistic and masochistic tendencies. Traditionally the male has symbolically represented the sadistic (warrior) side of the sadomasochism duo and the female the masochistic, suffering martyr.

Sadomasochism in sex may consist of the enjoyment of biting or playful slapping, or it may involve the extreme use of whips, canes, or other pain-inflicting devices to provoke sexual excitement. Fantasies concerning such extreme sadomasochistic sex are not common, and actual sadomasochistic behavior is even less frequent.

In general, more men than women in the United States are sadomasochists, and most sadomasochists stress their masochistic sides. Two principal explanations for the enjoyment of such sex are that people are psychologically conditioned to associate pain with sex, or they find infliction of pain useful in "releasing" suppressed sensory responses and feelings. People who find that pain aids their arousal probably first associated pain with sex in their early years. For example, a boy spanked when caught masturbating may associate the spanking with the illicit pleasure. Often when children are turned over a parent's knees for spanking their positioning may lead to tumescence in their genital areas, resulting in pleasurable sexual feelings simultaneous with the pain of the punishment. Not surprisingly, sadomasochistic fantasies and practices are more prevalent in cultures where corporal punishment of children is common.

Girls who are shown little affection by their fathers but receive physical punishment such as spanking may in their adult years associate male love and attention with dominance and infliction of pain. This kind of association, of course, can also affect boys who are similarly disciplined by a parent.

A child might grow up seeing the mother physically abused by the father, or have a mother who constantly plays the suffering role, and the youngster may either identify with the mother's masochistic role or take on its sadistic counterpart.

In many cultures, puberty initiation rites, especially for the male, incorporate pain. To become a man a boy has to show his bravery and not give in to or acknowledge the pain inflicted. To be a man is to be sexual; to be a man is to be able to withstand pain. In our own culture, men often associate violence and sex in their less formal initiation rites. A man from rural Kentucky recalls that the first time he felt like a man was when, at the age of 13, a rifle was given to him. A boy in the ghetto comes of age when he packs a knife or pistol. Boys who experienced their first intercourse at a neighborhood gang bang, or with a prostitute, also carry with them a violent—or at least nonloving— association with sex.

Many masochistic associations can be traced to early learning that sex is dirty, sinful, painful—a conjugal duty a woman must endure and that a man must inflict. Pain during sex can be the subconscious punishment the "sinner" believes to be mandatory. Some masochists are actually "secret sadists" who for some reason don't want to be the aggressor and inflict pain on another. So, as pain is being inflicted on them, they identify with the sadists. The sensations of pain and pleasure can be very close.

Many have in some way numbed their senses so they are not as sharp or responsive as they might be. Alcohol and cigarettes are the most popular "numbing" habits. Tranquilizers and other drugs do the job as well. As a depressant, alcohol anesthetizes some feelings; for example, an inebriated person loses acuity in his sense of touch. People who stop subjecting their taste buds to smoking speak of how all their senses become sharper. They become more emotional; food has more taste. They even become more sensitive to cigarette smoke itself, finding butts in an ashtray distasteful or their eyes and nasal membranes irritated by smoke. Nonsmokers say sex is more pleasurable than in their smoking days, and claim they have heightened sensual capability. Even orgasms are more intense, they claim.

Within our society the male especially is encouraged to suppress his emotional and physical sensitivities. He must remain steadfast and stoic through all pain and adversity. Often he pushes his true feelings and senses so far back inside that even when he wants to release them he can't. Therefore, for some, pain seems to provide the shock or abrupt incentive to feel and to let go, the prerequisites for good sex.

Quite obviously, it isn't the only and probably not the best method of dealing with sensory numbness or suppression. But it is a way some open themselves to sexual pleasure. Bondage is another.

Bondage—restraining someone or being restrained—is often, but not always, associated with sadomasochistic activities. Some people feel a special and even sexual excitement in being restrained. They like to have someone taunt them sexually and overtake them in their "helpless" position. This excitement of being held down and trying to "break free" is experienced by all of us to some degree. But those who want to be overcome sexually while restrained often prefer the passive role so they won't have to take personal responsibility for the sexual act. This is especially true of women raised in the madonna-prostitute tradition. If they are restrained in some way and sexually "acted upon" they can't be blamed for their participation. Male homosexuals who have for years suppressed and fought back their homosexual fantasies may also have a penchant for being bound. For even after "coming out," they may still require bondage to be sexually aroused.

Those who increase their sexual arousal by tying up and restraining their partners do so for many reasons. Generally, their need to control the other person is strong, and restraint is a tangible expression of this need; or restraint of one's partner might be a symbolic attempt to keep from being rejected or left alone. One young man showed insight into his own fears of being abandoned:

> The other fantasy of mine has me coming across a girl tied to a chair or bed. I enter, fondle the girl, release her, whereupon she (being excessively excited) jumps on me and we make passionate (what other kind?) love. I wouldn't like to experience this fantasy because I'd release her first, and she'd probably split fast.

We all symbolically bind and commit ourselves as we go through life. The institution of marriage is a classic example. Bondage in sex can sometimes symbolize a person's contradictory desires to be committed or bound to another in intimacy yet, at the same time, to "break free" from emotional or physical restraints.

The following masturbatory fantasies are concerned with sadomasochistic activities or bondage. Some men harbor such fantasies in secret while others act on them and go on to dream of new possibilities:

> One interesting fantasy is where I have a device that sexually stimulates people generally, sonically, or subliminally. I either use this on a group of people and observe and empathize with the resultant orgy, or I am with a woman I lusted after and lay back and enjoy her frantic seduction of me. This fantasy I might enjoy experiencing, except for the fact I analyze this fantasy into sadomasochistic and isolationistic attitudes and get rather embarrassed.

•

I fantasize about fist fucking another man. I've done it once and really dug it. Don't think I'd want some dude to put his fist up my ass though.

•

All of my thoughts while jacking off are of a S&M, B&D nature. In all of them the women involved are wearing costumes of leather, rubber chains, heavy make-up, long gloves, and always very high heels on their boots. Either all or long portions of the fantasies take place in public places: bars, parks, large gatherings of people.

It begins, as a rule, with my meeting a very beautiful, small, thin woman. She is attracted to me also and we go to my house. I dress her from my collection of B&D costumes (I have them for real) and while doing so we have sex in the forms of eating each other and then me fucking her to orgasm. When I have dressed her we go out to a bar and enter separately and sit apart. I then sit back and watch while she shows off and teases the other men in the place. She flashes her pussy, flirts with her tongue and eyes, and, while dancing with those who ask, whispers to them about having sex with them. Any and all of them who respond with requests or demands for normal sex she shuns. When she finds one that responds only to the way in which she is dressed and requests submission to her, she signals me and I let her know that he is suitable. She then leaves with him and I follow. When we get him to the car I handcuff him, and as I drive he is forced to watch while she sucks me off. This can also be seen by other people we pass. We take him to a quiet part of a park or into the country. I chain him to a tree and she whips and tortures him while she and I have all forms of sex with him watching. He is not allowed to touch himself but comes from the pain she offers and from watching us. We leave him tied in such a way that he can in a little while get away and we leave. I take her back home and punish her, telling her it is for the way she acted. The pain is real but in no way serious or lasting. With her bound tightly, I then take my pleasure with her and her body, using her in any way I want without regard for her feelings. I use her in such a way as to arouse her but am always careful not to allow her release. Finally, when she is really begging me to make her come I release her and then fuck and eat her until she has had so many orgasms that she again is forced to beg me to stop. It is while thinking about it really getting her off that I come myself.

I would as a rule have this full and complete fantasy when I'm home alone. I might have minor, shortened versions anywhere and anytime that I could take the chance to jack off. It could and does overlap into all of the other situations described, with the least likely being during actual sex. I have experienced the entire thing many times with the exception that the woman involved was not a stranger to me but was in fact my wife prior to her death. We acted this and other things out whenever we had the opportunity.

11

Personal Questions

WHAT WERE THE MOST EXCITING AND ENJOYABLE LOVEMAKING EXPERIENCES?

A woman who had been a long-standing friend came into town recently. I hadn't seen her for a long time. She's 44 years old, petite, and extremely ladylike— dainty, sophisticated, and the type that gives most people the impression that sex is the farthest thing from her mind. She came to town. I went to her mother's house to pick her up and stopped at the office to pick up something. In the office we just got to talking and playing and the level of play steadily progressed until we could no longer contain ourselves. We made love on the floor (well-carpeted) of the conference room in the dark. The conference room was dark 'cause it had no windows.

The lovemaking was exciting because of the spontaneity (some of the better experiences are spontaneous) and just the general excitement. There was a certain anxiety about the prospect of being caught. (It was a Saturday afternoon, and sometimes staff come to the office to catch up on work.) We could hear the elevator coming up and I listened to see if it would stop on our floor. One time it did—but the person went farther down the hall.

•

My most exciting, pleasurable sexual experiences happened in situations where we could have been caught any minute—like in public. Concern about being seen provokes a real high.

I was studying at the local university and somebody walked in that looked appealing. (We knew each other.) We looked for an empty classroom. The only available one was overlooking a seminary where some Jesuits were living.

Or if you're at somebody's house and their parents are at home, it's challenging to sneak in the room and get it on with the constant threat of being caught.

It's also exciting to have sex outside somewhere, especially on the beach. The moonlight the ocean water gives is a great effect. But even if it's cloudy or windy the elements of nature are tremendous aids to good sex. Water is also a good inducer to thinking and making decisions.

•

About ten years ago, one of the most beautiful trips I've had—that was fantastic, it was utopia for me. I had sex with two ladies. They didn't participate with each other but one looked on as I had sex with the other. I had sex with one and then started with the other. It was like falling off a mountain, the first one pushed me off, then the other one pushed me on. I noticed one thing (which hadn't happened when I was with one person), after I reached a climax, I continued to stay hard. Then I went on to another climax and was still hard—it was fantastic.

•

I went to one of those wrestling sessions that they have in Los Angeles, where you pay so much money to go in and wrestle with one of the women there. It's $10 entrance fee. I tried to have sex with the woman I was wrestling with and found out that that would be another $30. So I paid my money and we had sex. You know something, she gave me my money back after it was over—and later on we met at a motel and continued.

•

The best time was making love in a hotel looking over a Caribbean beach. I was so relaxed. My attentions weren't divided and I wasn't worried about someone's husband coming home. I really don't enjoy sex in a chancy or dangerous environment. Once I couldn't even perform because I was in this apartment and didn't really have a total understanding of the situation around me, really couldn't wait to get the lovemaking over and get out.

IN WHAT UNUSUAL PLACES
HAVE YOU MADE LOVE?

Marcy and I once made it at a very proper and boring party. We slipped away to do a couple of hits on a joint (marijuana), and we fucked with her sitting on the sink.

•

I did it once in the back of a cab. We were coming back from a very horny flick and couldn't wait. I gave the driver five bucks to turn his mirror around and keep driving. My date threw her legs across my lap with me turned into her.

•

We were out in the sticks in Virginia one weekend and pulled off the road by a small country bridge. Peg sat up on the railing of this fence and wrapped her legs around me, with me standing in front of her.

It was tremendous. A pickup truck went by and we barely noticed.

•

We couldn't quite manage intercourse but we did just about everything else to each other in a train from Chicago to New York. It was the middle of the night and we had our white overcoats draped across like blankets. A hundred miles of masturbating each other while everyone around us dozed.

•

It was especially hot in the city one Sunday afternoon, and my wife and I were padding around the house bareass. She bent over for something in the kitchen, and I hoisted her up a little and went right in from in back of her. She kind of gasped and held on to the counter. We loved it; talked about it for weeks after.

•

Well, there was a vacation we took up in the mountains during which we fucked like bunnies. The best was in a canoe right in the middle of a big lake. The rocking was amazing to feel inside her. We later tried it in a hammock and it was good but not as much. Fucking in that canoe, that was spectacular.

•

When we were kids we used to get rubbers from out of a machine in the gas station, then take our girls up into the stairways of apartment houses. Way up, past the last floor of apartments, there were stairs leading out onto the roof. We'd do it there after necking a lot. The girl would take off her panties, but leave her blouse and skirt and all on—in case someone came by.

•

I did it standing up in the library stacks. She had one leg up around my waist. We nearly got caught. We were so faint and flushed we didn't hear some guy chugging toward us pushing one of those library carts. He nearly ran us down. We were so young and crazy hot to fuck we didn't miss a beat. Could care less.

•

We decided to take a nude swim in the pool and turned out all the lights and dove in. A marvelous sensation. We slithered against each other a little and were thoroughly pleased with ourselves. Pam got into an inner tube when she got tired and was just floating around lazily. I swam underwater until she was just above, then ran my tongue across her ass and clit. When I surfaced, she said, "Fuck me. Here." At first I didn't know exactly how. Finally I held on to the tube by her feet and let myself float up underneath her. The pool water was beautifully cool and we were real warm. I remember vividly the sensation of penetrating her, my hot penis, the cold water, her hot cunt. Memorable, I tell you.

•

During my second year of interning I fell for one of the head nurses. She was years older than me but gorgeous, one of those spunky types. Wouldn't give me the time of day until she messed up on the job in a minor but embarrassing way. But I covered her mistake. Damn if she didn't come into the on-call room, rouse me from sleep, and just grasp my cock. She undid my pants, took it out, flicked off the lights with her free hand, and went down on me in the most delicious way.

•

We screwed in the tub many times. We sat facing. I'd get inside her and then we'd stretch out against the far ends of the bathtub. The undulations, the water—mmmmmmmmmm.

•

On my office desk—on top of all kinds of papers—and even a corporate contract that had been signed an hour before.

•

The most unusual experience I guess I've had was making love on a beach in the Caribbean and being bitten by little mosquitoes—millions of mosquitoes. We were on a blanket in the sand and my feet were at the water's edge.

HOW HAVE EROTIC BOOKS AND MAGAZINES AFFECTED YOUR SEX LIFE?

I usually masturbate after reading books—fantasize about having affairs with the characters or about someone I did not make it with.

•

Very little.

•

Improved it.

•

Well, they remind me that it would be nice to be having sex at that moment rather than reading about it.

•

Not much with the exception of magazines which provide a "concrete real" person. They also accustomed me to the idea of oral sex.

•

Brought to light erotic ideas that I hadn't really thought about or knew about, i.e., gimmicks and sexual paraphernalia.

•

They made me much more comfortable in discovering that other men's fantasies and sex lives parallel mine.

•

Hardly.

•

They try to make you believe that all girls look and act that way. I think some do in some ways but aren't all that free or eager. Yet I hope to find one or two that look that good like in *Playboy* or *Penthouse* and are that free.

•

They add fuel to the fire.

•

I use them during masturbation.

•

Probably not at all.

•

On those occasions when I rarely do read such books, I try to project myself into the story.

•

They've enriched it and made it more varied.

•

Very little. The person I'm with at a certain time has affected my sex life the most.

•

The most arousing parts I retain, reread, fantasize on.

•

While some are arousing they rarely add to sexual gratification.

•

They haven't to any great extent—perhaps in my earlier years gave me new ideas to try.

•

They can be very educating.

HOW HAVE EROTIC MOVIES AFFECTED YOUR SEX LIFE?

I went to a pornographic film show once; it was arousing for a while, then became a bore.

•

I get some good ideas.

•

Some "no name" pornos I have found arousing, and they do add to my thoughts about oral, genital sex, and pleasant surroundings.

•

I learned new methods or techniques to try at home.

•

They haven't.

•

Sometimes a movie like *Deep Throat* will arouse me, sometimes not, but movies haven't significantly affected my sex life.

•

Ryan's Daughter was more sexually arousing to me than hard-core porno. I like movies about true love, a story where love and affection are depicted. I desire and fantasize about having oral sex or any kind of sex with the women in the film.

HOW DOES ALCOHOL OR MARIJUANA AFFECT YOU?

One or two drinks free me up—help me to get rid of some of my inhibitions. That's good. But any more drinking means that I have trouble getting an adequate erection or it won't stay very long. So a lot of drinking can hinder my performance physically.

•

A little bit of drinking makes me horny—a lot of drinking makes me impotent.

•

Since alcohol is a depressant, it numbs my sexual feeling and "depresses" my ability to perform. Grass, on the other hand, really seems to add to my enjoyment of sex—all feelings seem to be enhanced, and the ecstasy of orgasm is prolonged.

•

I drink alcohol very infrequently. But I do enjoy getting high—herb (marijuana) makes sex fantastic.

It's just a wonderful feeling, and I'm able to get hard again faster after an orgasm when I'm high.

•

Alcohol makes the whole act of sex more difficult physically; maybe it's alcohol in the blood. Some people say grass makes sex better, but I don't see any difference.

WHAT WAS YOUR FIRST SEXUAL EXPERIENCE?

Oh my God. It had to be when I was playing house—when I was about 4 or 5 years old with a girl the same age. In kindergarten a bunch of us went to one guy's home, and his sister let us make love to her. We were caught by the mother and sent home. We had heard about sex from the older boys—you know they'd talk about it out in the streets.

I grew up in East Orange, New Jersey. There was a white family around the corner from us. There was a little girl in the family who used to make love with the little boys around. She would say to the little white boy she could make love to him, but she couldn't with me 'cause her mommy said no.

•

My first experience with intercourse was when I was about 13. I went to visit a friend of mine, but she wasn't home. As I waited for her a maid (a child molester, I suppose) encouraged me to have sex with her. She told me to follow her into the bedroom and then took off all her clothes and said, "What do you think?" She helped me take off mine, and then instructed me to come to the bed and lie on top of her. Almost before I got inside her I came. And that was the end of that. She said, "Was that your first time?" I told her it was. "Better me than someone in the streets," she assured me.

•

I had my first time bought for me. It was my eighteenth birthday. Terrifying. A regular public event.

•

It was in my freshman year at college. She was a sophomore and had a car. We weren't allowed automobiles the first year. Anyway, we parked one night. Up until then we had kept to fondling and masturbating each other. But that night—with only a half hour to go before the women's dorm was locked up—we just couldn't stand it anymore and did it right there in the front seat.

•

Her father was out of town, and I went over early in the morning. She was in a playful mood and took me to her parents' room to show me their contraception. We got to talking. Heck, I knew before we got upstairs what would go down. Well, we got into some heavy stuff and wound up fucking right there in the master bedroom. We must have done it a dozen times. It was the first for both of us, and we just couldn't seem to get enough. She worried for months after about her old man noticing the missing rubbers.

•

Jesus, it was three days after the wedding. Martha had her period just about when the priest tied the knot. Just like her. It's been downhill from there ever since. I don't know how we managed the three kids we've got. That's not really true. It wasn't quite that bad. The first few years were hell. We just didn't know anything except what I had picked up on the streets. It was damn hard for both of us—embarrassing until we finally learned to laugh about it.

•

I was really quite old to be a virgin (23) and wasn't even sure I could function right since I'd had almost no dates in high school and college. I was very shy and considered myself to be unattractive.

I met Laura when I was helping to audit the accounts of the consulting agency she was working for. We talked a lot during those days I was at the office, and I was amazed with the comfort I started to feel with her. Eventually I asked her out to lunch. Then we started dating a couple times a week. It took a lot of courage to work up the nerve to kiss her. When I did I knew I'd done it all wrong, but she seemed to be interested in me. Finally after some hot petting in the car, we tried to make love. It was a fiasco. It was really horrible. Everything went wrong. I thought she'd never want to see me again. But somehow she did and we tried it again soon and it was an improvement. I found out she was as naive about sex as I was. But we were kind of patient with each other, and I think it was helpful. Also some of the sex books I was reading helped me understand more about foreplay and the possible varieties in a relationship. Laura and I went out for over a year and eventually drifted apart. But I feel that I was particularly lucky to have my first experience with such a caring, understanding person.

•

My first sexual experience was under a roll-away bed when I was 6 years old, with my cousin. I put my penis in her vagina and moved around 'cause I was told that was what you did when you fucked. She squealed as 6-year-old would do. But I don't think either of us had an orgasm. It was just fun.

•

My first experience was in the basement of a tenement building. I was about 8 or 9 at the time and went into my first perverted act. I was playing house with a girl and decided to go into the bathroom to take a leak. She suggested I use her mouth as a receptacle. I obliged, but found that when I put my penis in her mouth I couldn't take a leak 'cause she was sucking the shit out of it. So I had my first oral sex. I didn't ejaculate 'cause I guess I was still too young. But I sure enjoyed it. It was a fall day and the warmth of her lips on my johnson was great. When I think of it—my God—she was a pro at such a young age.

•

My parents are the liberal sort. Very open-minded. Sally was actually allowed to stay over in my room. Dad even provided me with a contraceptive, but it proved unnecessary as she informed me that she was on the pill.

DO YOU PREFER TO HAVE SEX WITH AN OLDER OR YOUNGER WOMAN?

Young chicks are tighter. They just have better bodies. Older women, on the other hand, are more experienced, know how to move, aren't put off by what men like and aren't afraid to ask. They appreciate you more also. I like both. Older women don't turn you on so quickly, but they take you off beautifully.

•

I'm inclined toward the more youthful, unjaded female. She is not as programed; she's fresher. I also think I like their naiveté. It's provocative. I love to introduce her, say, to oral sex. Very arousing the idea of their experiencing it for the first time, and going down on someone for the first time—me.

•

It's really hard for me to be loose with somebody really young. Making love to them is real fine. Having them do it to me is something else. With an old chick I can give in, submit, and enjoy it.

•

I like to be with both younger and older women (I'm 31). But if I had to choose I'd definitely choose older women. Probably if I was put on a couch, someone would say it's because of the lack of attention from my mother when I was a child. Now there are different things I like about younger women—their youthfulness, adventurous nature, free spirit, and the fact that for a lot of the things in sex that's the first time she's done it before.

The fact that I consider myself to be older mentally than my years automatically directs my interest to older women. They know what they want. An older woman is experienced sexually, which is a big thing to me. She's more sensitive than a younger woman and generally more established. I mean especially the career types, and I like an ambitious woman. Older women are just more sexually exciting to me altogether.

•

I sort of prefer older women (over 29), and am not opposed to women older than me for a variety of reasons. (I'm 39.) They're more knowledgeable, more considerate, and not so much in a hurry. They know the subtleties. (The younger ones just want to go bang bang, gymnastics, rather than expressions of feeling or enjoying themselves with another.) Older women are more sure of themselves and don't feel they have to put on a gymnastics show and aren't engaging in contests of power or will. They are more divested of a lot of fantasies. By having experienced more, they are more in touch with reality in terms of what to expect out of a man or what to give a man.

But it can work both ways. Older women who have had a lot of unfavorable experiences can be turned off and inhibited.

One of the best pieces I've ever had was a woman in her 50s. I thought she was 35. She looked great and took great care of her body; it was soft and smooth. She sure knew what to do.

•

There's an equal attraction. It seems to me if they're older, they should be ten or fifteen years older. (I'm 26.) Age never seems to be a major element. I just like women. I'm not too picky. In some respects older women may be partners whereas you have to serve as an instructor for younger women.

•

Having someone younger is special. Makes me feel very tender, somewhat nostalgic for my own salad days, yet at the same time it makes me feel a youth again.

•

I get off—truly go off—on balling two at a time, giving it to the young thing in the ass while sucking off the older one. And so on.

•

Real young women are irresistible. I don't know what I'm going to do when I hit 30. I worry a lot about what people would say about an old john bedding teenagers. There aren't many more seasons I can get away with it, when my baby-face looks give out.

•

Nice tight pussy is unbeatable, and you can only get it into your crib by robbing the cradle. They've gotta be young to have that kind of snatch.

•

When I was young I preferred older women who looked young, and now that I'm older (I'm 40) I prefer younger women who look older. I think maybe this is so because when I was young, I used to go to a nearby museum often and was interested and attracted to the buxom Romanesque women represented there in sculpture and paintings, and as I looked around in real life, it seemed that the older women had this quality.

Now I like the vitality of younger women but like them to act or appear to have the maturity of older women.

•

I fantasize about young women, not teenagers, and wonder how it might be to engage in sex with a couple who work in my office. (They're in their early 20s.)

It's not really the age thing as much as sensuality in a person.

I do like making love to older women. I find it's comfortable, relaxing and not a hassle. There's no real demand (which is real, being married) and they're interesting. Sex is a very important part of my life, but I enjoy companionship and conversation. I like to learn from people, and older women are challenging mentally as well as physically.

I've made love to a lot of older women. God. They're very appreciative too. And people like to feel appreciated.

•

In some respects older women make better partners, because with younger women you end up being an instructor.

HOW DO YOU APPROACH A WOMAN FOR THE FIRST TIME?

I play it by ear—you can't force it. I tell people I'm no hassle. I truly believe it takes two in bed—I'd never physically or mentally force someone. You can pick up sexual feelings—the immediate decision comes through the girl's experience. If she's inexperienced, I have to be more gentle, almost a pretended naiveté on my part.

•

I have what I call the four-month strategy. I get to know the young woman and to be her friend. I don't try anything sexual. It's amazing how it works. I have never been turned down. After being friends for four months, she's almost trying to seduce me. I guess she feels comfortable with me and doesn't feel pursued or that she has to be on the defensive. When we do have sex it's usually very exciting 'cause it's built up over a long time, and I really don't feel that I have to make that one great impression the first time in bed because I also feel more comfortable with her and sure of our ongoing relating.

•

I find it very awkward and scary to try to get a girl in bed. I usually do the regular old stuff—take her out for dinner, dancing, maybe a movie or play. Then I try to sense if she's ready. I must admit I'm not a very good judge. I know the extreme cases, but most girls confuse me. They either get irritated when I make moves on them or pissed off and think something's funny with me if I don't.

•

I go through the warming-up routine, try to hold her hand at first, then kiss her at the appropriate time—you know, when it's kind of private. You can usually tell by how she acts when you kiss her if she's interested in more. If her kisses are passionate I suggest that we go for a nightcap to her place. Then I just let nature take its course.

•

I really don't have any system of seducing a woman. You can usually tell if someone is interested. I wait till all the vibes are right. I think if you try to be sensitive you can pick up signals about where she's at—words, body language. I don't go with that old "macho" theory that when a woman says "no" she means "yes." A woman will communicate her feelings to you if you allow it. In the ol' days I think a lot of women felt they had to resist a sexual encounter 'cause they'd be considered in a bad light if they gave in. It was just a conquering game by the man. I try not to go at things like that. If a woman doesn't want to sleep with me I try not to let it get to me. Hell, not everybody's attracted to everybody else. I'm sure Robert Redford's been turned down too.

Personal attraction's a funny thing. There are many women I wouldn't choose to sleep with, so I assume it works both ways.

•

I just try to be frank with the girl. I don't want to waste her time or mine. If I want to fuck her I just say so—that way we aren't into game playing and she'll certainly come back with her own frank answer.

DOES THE SIZE OR SHAPE OF A WOMAN'S VAGINA AFFECT SEX?

Of course it does—but so many other things do too. It also depends on what the guy's penis is like. Generally men prefer tight, close-fitting vaginas—but if a man has a big penis he might want a bigger vagina.

•

You know, unless the size is extreme in some way— either large or small—I don't think it really matters much.

•

I have trouble with coming too soon—and if a woman's real tight—it's a problem for me. So I like looser women.

•

Jesus, I was with this one woman, and she was so big it was like being in a cave just looking for a wall to get a little friction with. Too big—don't like 'em so big you just slush around.

•

I have a rather large penis, and if I'm with a woman with a tight or small vagina, sometimes she can't stretch enough for me. I can't get all the way in and it's painful for her. I prefer women with more room inside.

•

I like my lover's vagina to fit me like a glove—tight and soft—moving as I move.

HOW DO YOU MAKE LOVE TO A WOMAN? IS THERE A PATTERN, A CONSISTENT TECHNIQUE YOU MOSTLY USE?

I'm afraid so. I usually start out kissing her lips, neck, shoulder, ear, then her breasts and nipples, on down to her stomach, careful not to tickle her. If I think she'll not be embarrassed or insulted, I'll go down on her for a short while, touch her inside to check that she's wet enough, try to turn her on more that way, and go in when she signals. It wasn't until recently that I realized how regimented the whole process had become.

•

I try to be spontaneous and sort of let our vibrations and communication tell what to do. Each woman is different—each time is different.

•

No, I have no set procedure. I'm into a lot of different stuff. Like oils and massages. Beverly, I would massage her for days. She'd look like an otter. Then I'd oil my joint and slide in from behind, bracing myself on the sides so as not to slip off. Powerful stuff that oil. Silky, man. Ever try it on a water bed? Unbelievable.

•

I don't use any special techniques. It varies depending on the situation, the woman, how I feel, a lot of variables. I'm fairly consistent in the things I do— the whole foreplay bit, stimulation of her tongue, fingers, touching, stroking of the body and all that— the various positions during intercourse and different ways of stroking. But the timing may change with the situation—and the sequence may change as well.

•

Yeah, there's a standard warm-up. Beforehand I always figure out something new, but as I get turned on I can't seem to remember the new thing and fall back on the old thing. Damn.

•

No, no preliminaries. If she's hot enough to want it I figure she's ready and I just put it to her. Haven't had any complaints.

•

I like to swing into the room on a chandelier. No seriously. If I have a routine, I'm not conscious of it. I'm just not the type. I like sex without anxiety. For instance, oh, putting a condom inside her and trying to get into it while she's holding the rim. Doesn't work worth a shit but it's a lot of laughs trying. I like unserious sex.

•

My approach was pretty dull I was told. I used to start out with a coy massaging of my old lady's shoulders. I'll work up under her blouse, cup her, slip the top off her shoulders, undress her real slow. Too slow, she said, too long and overdramatic.

•

Don't be so mechanical was her message—constantly. Let yourself go, get behind it, expand out into yourself, touch your borders and push out beyond. Groaning would help, she said. Fuck. Every time I was unmechanical I lost all control, came too fast, pooped out early. I'd be half asleep through most of it. I sought outside help; got us a water bed. Some help. So I'd be half out and seasick and worrying all the time that it would bust out from under us or we'd fall off while it was slushing us around. A bad scene. The Victorians had it easier.

•

Used to have a regular check list when I was younger, primarily because I was so scared, I guess. I got better gradually and loosened up.

HOW DO YOU FEEL ABOUT
WOMEN'S ORGASMS?

I wish I knew when my wife has an orgasm. She says that's not important to know and she usually tells me. But I'm confused. Sometimes she says she had an orgasm, and I've felt her contractions. Other times she says she's had one and I don't feel them. Is she lying to me or are her physiological signs so diverse there's no one way for me to tell?

•

I read in a sex book that you can tell when a woman has an orgasm because her nipples get hard. I used to try to casually feel my partner's nipples to see. But several women have told me that that's no indicator—hard nipples just basically mean aroused, not necessarily orgasm.

•

I can tell if a woman has had an orgasm if her lips are cold after.

•

For years I've been trying to find out the real sign of a woman's orgasm. Sometimes I can tell by the way her body moves back and forth and the vagina squeezes me. Other times I'm not sure, and I don't think the women I've been with are completely honest with me.

•

When my girlfriend has her orgasm, she grips on and pulls my penis with her vagina. She gets so into it that I usually have an orgasm at the same time.

•

I resent not knowing when a woman has an orgasm. That's the ultimate secret and one that men can't share and can't have themselves—since it's obvious when a guy is turned on and when he comes.

•

I don't really care whether or how many times a woman comes. It's up to her. Her enjoyment is the important thing—not an orgasmic scorecard. I just want us to enjoy together. I'd do whatever feels good to her.

Most men expressed a fascination in a woman's capacity to multi-orgasm in a relatively short period of time. Several men said they are envious of this.

I wish I could have the quick, multi-orgasmic capability that a woman has.

•

I resent women for being able to have so many orgasms in a limited amount of time. I want to do the same. And I feel I have to help them do and enjoy what I cannot.

•

I'll tell you the truth. Sex is getting too complicated. Sometimes I just go and pay a prostitute so I don't have to worry about "fulfilling" the women—the ones who don't enjoy sex and just put you off and the nymphomaniacs who can't ever get enough. I'm tired of both. Now suddenly having an orgasm has become so important to many women that they expect you to do anything you can—standing on your head if you have to—to make sure they get off.

WHAT DOES A VAGINA FEEL LIKE?

Like a warm, very moist, very soft haven.

•

It's wet and warm—some women are tight like a glove. Others are big—you feel like you're in a dark warm cave and you press against the moist warm walls.

•

Like a warm piece of meat—a steak all around.

•

Like silk. Actually there're a lot of different feelings. Some women have a sturdy structure around their soft vaginal walls. Other women are not so firm. Some women are deep and open inside, other women are shorter, but they loosen up with activity and sometimes seem like they open wide as they start to climax.

•

There's nothing like a good, warm pussy. Nothing. Except maybe a hot pussy. Women do get different temperatures. I guess the more turned on—the hotter they are. Also, the wetter they are. Don't like a dry pussy.

•

It feels secure and pleasurable. Good. Just very delightful. Like soft warm water. There's nothing else like it to compare it with.

DO YOU LIKE THE WOMAN TO BE ACTIVE DURING LOVEMAKING? TO THRUST AND MOVE?

My wife wouldn't know from moving. It's all she can do just to keep breathing while it's being done.

•

I love it when she does the moving. It's the one time I know exactly when she's coming. I mean I can feel her build up to it, feel her nearing it, then fading a little, then reaching that point again, and finally being caught by the wave and swept along in a frenzy.

•

Meg has never been shy—thank God—about being active. Yes, I very much enjoy her participation. In fact, I've noticed in the last few years that I may actually prefer her assuming the dominant role in initiating our coupling and directing it. I'm blessed with a brazen mate and it is wonderful. Lately I have come to suspect this is true of many men in their mid-life. That they prefer a very active, if not dominating, partner.

•

I like the woman to move and be active in sex. Who wants to be with a wet dishrag? Plus, we should be working together. It's a partnership, not just me moving around. I get tired sometimes, and when a woman takes part she is giving me feedback about what she likes, and I can have her do some of the things I like.

•

It turns me on when a woman moves. I feel she's really into what we're doing.

•

Sometimes I dig it, if the chick knows what she's about. It can get out of hand, however. Mostly I like to be the boss and do the servicing. There is one who's particularly good that way. The things she knows! She's got more moves than O.J. And she's fantastic giving me head.

•

I think the intensity, or at least the excitement, of the orgasm is enhanced by an active woman—especially the kind who knows how to thrust at the right time.

•

I like women to do everything. I like to feel that it's my show, but also like to give up the lead position and trade. I get tired. Shit, I'm getting old. I like the woman to move, but not frantically, or in a way I'd bounce out. That's disconcerting. Then we have to stop so I can get back in.

•

I get turned on by active and very turned off by inactive women who just lie there like a receptacle.

The more active the better. I like a woman to attack me.

•

I like it really hard, you know? And few women do it hard enough to suit me, and the ones that do I don't like because the way they hump it really is banging. Too hard, if you know what I mean.

•

She's got to do some of it if she's really going to get off. Besides a man's got to have some rest.

DO YOU PREFER ORAL OR GENITAL SEX?

I prefer oral sex. It's a more intense pleasure. I used to have trouble ejaculating in someone's mouth. But I overcame it; it used to bother me. I still tend to pull out, but some partners don't want you to. There's a fear that somehow I'll be drained.

•

Genital sex, of course—oral is nice and sort of focuses at one point. But by far the best orgasms can happen when two people who really dig each other make love.

•

Oral sex is quite a treat and a diversion, but if the partner's right and the situation, coming in her can be pure heaven.

•

I think in oral sex there's a great deal more of a feeling of power. The woman is being submissive in carrying out oral sex. It's a combination of a sense of power (and also depends on the abilities of the individual). If she's good, it's like watching an artist at work. I watch instead of closing my eyes 'cause it adds something to the experience. I can orgasm with my eyes open. In fact I prefer it.

•

Both are very nice. I prefer the genital sensations in most instances. Maybe once or twice in my whole life I experienced orgasm through oral stimulation. I like oral sex as part of a process—getting to genital sex—but not just in itself.

DO YOU PREFER A CERTAIN WAY OR POSITION TO ATTAIN ORGASM DURING INTERCOURSE?

I've got to go in from behind. I think it's physical, but lately I've come to think it's psychological. There's something funky about doing it that way that gets me.

•

Any way I can get it is fine with me.

•

I like all positions but especially with my partner straddling me, touching my balls, my penis hitting her vagina front and back as she moves back and forth.

•

My wife has a very large vagina, and I find it difficult to come in any position. I mean it's great. However, after she has come, she'll usually disconnect and suck me off. For a long time she thought I minded this. I don't, honestly. She's great at fellatio.

•

I love being on top and moving real easy, pulling back until I'm almost out of her, making her crazy till she moves to get me all back inside. Gets me every time, much more than thrashing around.

•

I like to start sitting up with Deb on my lap. Then we lay back away from each other and I fondle her clit. It's tricky staying in her but worth the effort. She doesn't like it as much, though. Says I'm too far away.

WHAT DO YOU LIKE YOUR PARTNER TO DO DURING LOVEMAKING?

I had a great orgasm by accident several years ago and since then like to have my partner duplicate this. The woman I was with had an electric vibrator and wanted to come by putting it on top of her clitoris while I had my penis inside of her. Very soon I realized that this was very exciting for me, too. The vibration was exceptionally stimulating. After my partner had her orgasm I stayed inside without moving. Very soon the vibration made me have an uncontrollable and intense orgasm. Who says only women can enjoy vibrators?

•

After orgasm I like to have her gently rub or scratch my back.

•

After orgasm I like her to be close and to hold me as I hold her. I don't like for the woman to immediately jump up to wash.

•

Just as I'm getting ready to have an orgasm, I like my partner to rub or suck on my tits. This is easiest to do if she's on top of me.

•

As I'm getting ready to come, my wife slaps my rear cheeks. This makes the climax more intense.

•

When my partner is on top of me and I start to climax, I like her to shove her finger up my ass.

•

I like my partner to sit on me and as I start to come give me a "golden shower" [i.e., urinate].

After men get over the fear of having their testicles hurt, they often find gratification in having them touched and rubbed by their partner.

During foreplay, I like to have my partner scratch the underneath part of my testicles. She pulls my balls up toward my penis and scratches the underneath part—not in a painful, hurting way—but in a stimulating way as someone might scratch a dog.

•

As she is giving me head, I like her to gently take my testicles in her mouth and gently suck and lick—and even blow a little on each one.

•

I like for my partner to push and rub firmly with her hand—starting from underneath my balls, flattening my balls against the base of my penis and pushing until her hand reaches my penis and grasps it. Then she can start over again.

•

While she's sucking my penis—I get very turned on when my wife takes some honey and puts it all over my penis and my balls. It's especially stimulating when she sucks the lower back part of my penis and gently sucks and licks the honey off my balls.

ARE THERE SPECIAL THINGS YOU LIKE YOUR PARTNER TO DO WHILE GIVING YOU ORAL SEX?

I like her to put my penis, deep, deep, inside her mouth and throat.

•

I want my partner to put my complete penis in her mouth and to go up and down—striking the right rhythm as I move my body to help the motions.

•

It drives me wild to have a woman open her throat wide and move my penis in and out. Linda Lovelace is a dream come true for many men.

•

I want to be swallowed—my penis going deep into her throat and my come eventually released deep inside her.

•

I like to have the head of my penis tantalized before she actually puts my penis deep in her mouth. I like for her to lick and tease the head with her tongue.

•

A strong sucking motion on my penis—especially the top part—is very exciting. I feel like the semen is being pulled to the top of my penis and ready to burst out at any time.

•

My girlfriend starts giving me head by sucking in a circle around the "fringe" of my penis—the part just below the head—she goes around until I beg her to engulf my whole penis in her mouth.

•

When she sucks my penis and goes in an up-and-down motion. I like for my partner to hold the lower part of my penis tightly in her hand. It increases the intensity of the pleasure I'm receiving.

•

Most men don't seem to like this, but I enjoy having my penis gently skimmed with my partner's teeth as she's on the up motion—until she gets to the head—then I like her to suck hard and start over again.

•

While she's going up and down on my penis with her mouth, I like for my partner to push my thighs apart, as if she's trying to get to my most protected part. I will act as if I'm resisting her—but she will prevail.

•

When I'm getting head I like the woman to play with me and put her finger—or another object—in and out of my ass with the same rhythm as she's sucking me.

•

I like the woman to make me come and to swallow the semen.

•

I don't know why, but it is an extreme turn-on to have my wife carry out oral sex on me in this way. She covers me with a black cotton cloth that has a hole in it so my penis can protrude out. Otherwise, I'm fully covered to my neck. She then plays with my penis with her hands, and puts it between her breasts before inserting it in her mouth. When she gets it in her mouth she puts it deep in then exposes almost the whole penis—then deep, etc. I get so turned on by watching. Something about the contrast of my white/pinkish penis—and her white skin and blond hair against that black cloth is very exciting. Also, it is almost as if my penis is isolated—a sexual symbol—sexy and exciting—not even a part of my body. White semen shooting up and dropping on the black cloth is the grand aesthetic finale.

•

It sounds crazy, but it's very stimulating to have the woman hum as she gives me head. One woman I have sex with can do that, and it almost feels like a vibrator. It is also exciting when she holds a vibrator against my penis and balls as she sucks me.

CIRCUMCISION—DOES IT MATTER OR NOT IN SEXUAL RELATIONS?

I was circumcised as a baby so I don't know what it feels like to be uncircumcised. I've heard though that the pleasure isn't as great.

•

I'm not circumcised, but I feel orgasm intensely. In fact, sometimes the intensity is so strong when the skin is pulled back and the tip of my penis is exposed it is painful. I use "numbing" cream so this won't be a problem. I keep myself clean, so I don't see that not being circumcised is a problem. In fact, I'd feel like an important part of me were missing if that foreskin were trimmed.

•

I'm not circumcised and enjoy sex very much. Women I've been with have said it's a turn-on to push the skin back and expose the rest of my penis—sort of like a dog's penis as it emerges from hiding.

•

I was circumcised when I was 28 for two reasons: because I heard it was more hygienic and might help prevent any possibilities of cancer, but mainly because the skin was connected over the tip of my penis and it was sometimes painful during intercourse 'cause the skin was pulled so tightly. For me, circumcision meant much better sex—in fact, I really believe my penis gets bigger now because it doesn't have the skin at the top to impede its enlargement. Also, I feel much freer now during sex—probably because I don't have to worry about possible pain.

•

Women have told me they prefer circumcised men because they can see more of the head of the penis. Also, some women have heard that sex with an uncircumcised man may cause cervical cancer. I think research has recently challenged this theory. But generally, it's easier to keep clean when you're circumcised.

WHAT TYPE OF CONTRACEPTION DO YOU PREFER?

I really hadn't used rubbers for a long time, but do now because my wife stopped taking pills. She wanted me to have a vasectomy. I didn't want to. The rubber does take away some of the spontaneity in sex 'cause you have to stop to put it on. It doesn't inhibit me at all. I don't notice any loss in feeling or enjoyment. My wife does, but she doesn't want to get pregnant.

Diaphragms are OK. Women I make love to usually have them in already (so we don't have to stop). It amazes me. They either somehow know we're going to make love or else walk around with their diaphragms in all the time.

I had sex with a woman who had an I.U.D. once and could feel it scraping. It hurt and I was concerned and didn't want to hurt myself.

Foam is messy and inconvenient.

But none of those contraceptives make that much difference in the feeling. I especially don't mind rubbers. The important thing is that people effectively use contraceptives, and there is a special joy in having sex with a person who shares with you the responsibility of avoiding unwanted pregnancy. That planning and responsible sharing are far more important than inconveniences of using contraceptives.

•

I really don't prefer any, but of course contraception is a necessary evil, better than unwanted pregnancies or abstinence, I'll tell you that.

Condoms take the feeling away—like taking a bath with a raincoat on. They also interrupt the continuity, and it's embarrassing having to stop and put one of those things on. The dude starts to lose his erection while fumbling with the rubber.

I can feel a diaphragm, and it prohibits my intrusion, I don't like it.

I'm afraid the I.U.D. might get caught on my tongue or my johnson.

Foam—yuck. It usually precludes oral sex, just can't do it with foam, like eating shaving cream.

I'm too egotistical for a vasectomy and don't get enjoyment with condoms. Wish there was a good birth-control method for men. If there was a pill available for men, I'd take it. It wouldn't bother me at all, matter of fact I'd probably welcome it.

•

The fucking I.U.D. and the safe [condom] bother me. Diaphragms aren't too bad. I'm not crazy about them. Foam is a bit messy, but can be useful when a woman can't lubricate.

Once when having sex with a woman who was wearing an I.U.D. I could feel the wire. I don't know if it was installed wrong. I was always bumping into the thing. Once I think I sort of got bruised on the side.

•

Anything that has to do with the male bothers me. I refuse to use one. It goes against my principles.

Most everybody I've dealt with, they're using the pill, or else I can't tell. I usually assume they're taking care of themselves.

•

Neither the I.U.D. nor the diaphragm bother me. I can't even feel them. It's like it's not there. No problem.

•

It's okay but it's a real drag if she has to replenish the jelly later on. It's also no fun to go down on somebody wearing one. The jelly smells like a hospital and tastes worse.

Pill

Obviously, I can't feel any sensation. However, I talked my wife out of taking the pill because I couldn't stand thinking about the risks involved. It's too drastic chemically and simply dangerous. I don't care if the odds are a million to one. I'm married to a woman who is one in a million.

•

I didn't think much about them at first. Joyce would pop one every morning and that was that, until I noticed small changes. She got irritable, a little heavier. Not for us, I told her. She went back to her diaphragm.

•

I thought *finally* when they first came out. Seven years later Milly got a blood clot in her lung and the doc took her off the pill.

•

Terrific, if you're not the one taking them. They must find something better soon. Until then, it's the mechanical means for us.

Condoms

Not much fun in the old days. In fact, I used to think the government deliberately advocated them out of puritanical spite. I couldn't believe the technological power of the U.S. couldn't produce a decent male contraceptive. However, the new ones aren't so bad. They're made out of natural skin.

•

Lousy things, rubbers. I've been down on them forever. The first time I tried to use one I caught my pubic hair in the band. Pain you wouldn't believe. And being young and stupid, I wouldn't stop in the middle of balling.

•

They're terrible except for the special ones with ribs and stuff. I didn't believe they really worked for a woman until I tried it myself. So now occasionally I use one, but not really for contraception.

•

God-awful. They feel like contraceptives might have been meant to feel.

•

I think a priest must have invented them during the Inquisition.

•

I like to use them because they reduce the sensation just enough for some to last a long time. There's one woman I have to use them with, she takes so long to come.

I.U.D.

It's fine for me but I couldn't stand watching Judy going through all the convulsions in getting adjusted to it.

•

I can feel the string. I don't like them.

•

My wife had it in wrong and it really jammed me one time. Ouch.

•

No problem. I don't even know it's there.

Foam

Messy stuff.

•

I didn't care until I found I was allergic to it. What a rash!

•

It has a very cold consistency and feels quite peculiar. Needless to say, it discourages one from getting into the act.

DO YOU OPEN OR CLOSE YOUR EYES DURING ORGASM? DURING MASTURBATION? DURING SEXUAL RELATIONS?

When I masturbate I usually keep my eyes open so I can watch the sperm shoot out. During intercourse I usually close my eyes.

•

When I masturbate I close my eyes when I'm using a fantasy or open them if I'm looking at an erotic picture, magazine, etc. During intercourse I do both —open and close depending on the situation.

•

During masturbation I close them—while making love I open them—it's a real turn-on to watch my partner's face when she's into the sex we're having.

•

The only time I close my eyes is when I sleep or sneeze.

•

During masturbation I close my eyes 'cause I fantasize. I might open them just as I ejaculate. During lovemaking I generally close my eyes—sometimes during a great orgasm I'll see visions of bright colors or stars exploding, etc.—couldn't see those with open eyes.

IN GENERAL WHAT DON'T WOMEN UNDERSTAND ABOUT MEN OR, SPECIFICALLY, WHAT DON'T WOMEN YOU KNOW UNDERSTAND ABOUT YOU?

Most women are pretty superficial in thinking that sex is the act that's going to keep the man going, and they don't think about what a man really wants. For example, some women think that if they let you have sex with them all other problems and needs will be solved for a man. It's much more complicated than that. I think women think sex is a simplistic solution for men.

Also it has always fascinated me that sex plays such an important part in a relationship. (It's OK to have friends of the opposite sex, but the partner goes crazy if you go to bed with one of them.) The irony is that something that's considered the core of a commitment is treated with so little innovation or creativity. A person doesn't know the all-and-all about sex the first time or even the five-hundredth time. Some people act like "automatically, I do it good." It's sort of automatic procreation. It should be something that is developmental, learning new ways and skills of relating constantly. A couple ought to grow in their sex experiences and explore together, changing the automatic to the dynamic.

•

Women don't understand that we are vulnerable, but we don't admit it. We hate to admit it. We hate to be told. And even though we'd like to be hardasses, we love to be around emotion—not hysteria, that's different. Emotion without craziness is gentle. It's cathartic—emotion.

Men have a tremendous yearning to open up to somebody, but they don't know how. Men don't know where to go with all the emotion they're feeling. There's great frustration at not being able to sort it out, and unchanneled anger. Many men, not recognizing this anger at its first level as self-anger, let it become haughtiness, or they become passive-aggressive—letting other people be angry for them.

When people don't understand what's going on in my life, I sometimes hold them responsible for not being sensitive enough. For example, if I'm concerned about something it's almost like I expect the woman I'm involved with to know what's on my mind. Men often expect women to be mind readers, and to respond correctly.

Most of the women I'm close to don't understand that I really want to have someone who can simultaneously support my successes and accept my failures—be honest.

•

The thing that women understand the least is a man's anxiety over the first sexual experience with a new partner. To the man it's usually the worst of the encounters. Christ, I really think so. At least it is to me. You're feeling each other out. The man is feeling anxiety over whether he's going to get it or not. Is it going to be good or not good? Am I going to like it? Is she going to like it? Lot of anxieties. Hope to put on a good enough show to get a second chance. Also you hope the other person is good.

Women who have been with me and tell me how I was the first time say it was so-so. But there was enough potential for a second going, and it gets better.

Many women don't adequately appreciate the importance of sex to the individual or the individual style—sexual personality. It would help if women appreciated a man's individual style and discerned enough about the style to develop an appropriate response.

Women don't understand the effect their response has on the outcome.

•

I wish the women I'm involved with would understand how horny I am in the mornings when I wake up. I always wake up with a hard penis and want sex very much—even if I had it the night before. Sometimes I wake up at five in the morning in this state. My partner doesn't want to have sex at this time. She usually wants to sleep to the last minute before she absolutely has to get up. It just seems like very poor timing. Here I am hard and ready to go and she's not into sex at all. In fact, she might be bothered 'cause she wants to sleep. What am I supposed to do? Take a cold shower, masturbate, go to work with a hard-on? Wish women would understand that men often wake up in this state and would make some kind of allowances or preparation for it.

•

I wish women would not always expect the man to be the aggressive one. I would like to be pursued every so often. I would like to be taken out to dinner or get a nice present—or have the woman drive the car on the date. Don't women understand it's not fun to always be the initiator?

•

From my standpoint, the women I know don't understand how busy I am and how much time I can spend with them. It's quality of the time spent with each other instead of quantity. I suppose this isn't a man/woman problem so much. I guess career women and other women also are very busy, but for some reason the women I date just want to spend more time with me than I can really afford.

•

Most of the women I've been involved with can't understand why I'm so brash and arrogant. They think I'm insensitive and really have no feelings. The truth is that I'm a big front, because deep down I'm a nice, lovable person. But the world is tough. I grew up on the streets, and although I'm a successful businessman now, it's no different. People will stab you in the back if they sense weakness. You have to have a mask to keep people off your ass. Many people expect a man to be tough, brash and hard, so I give it to them. But I can be tender and loving, too, if I don't get hurt by it. You'd be surprised how many women'll run you over if you try to be sensitive and show some feelings—sometimes the same ones that get upset because you come on so tough. When I meet a woman I like, I play it cool for a long time. I act like I'm not particularly interested and have her come after me. If I act interested or call her very often or stuff like that, the woman might lose interest or think I'm weak.

•

I don't like the pressure I feel from women to be a constant sexual stud. There are times I want sex, there are times I don't feel like it. But a lot of women seem to expect a man to walk around with a constant hard-on and always want sex. That's not me

210

and I bet other men feel the same way. Sometimes, I "have a headache."

•

So many men are confused since women's lib—the macho role doesn't work—they don't know how to be.

•

Most women don't understand the insecurity they give a man by faking orgasm. With a real orgasm there's convulsivity and spontaneity of the body. When I suspect that a woman I'm with has faked an orgasm, I'm virtually impotent (I may still be hard, but not really interested anymore).

•

I think the woman I'm involved with doesn't understand the basic thing that is important to me—and that's being trusted. She couldn't possibly realize the impact of a person that constantly mistrusts you.

•

Most women aren't aware of their own sexuality or what to do with it—and how a man is responding to it. A lot of women think of phony sexy stuff like what to wear, the "right" perfume, etc—they don't think of the real essence of sexuality.

•

I think that most women don't understand the sexual desires or drives of a man. Most women—of course, it's changing now—but most women in the past didn't feel like experimenting, or feel men should play the seductive role over women. It's kind of different to be with a woman that's equally aggressive as you are —I like it.

The hardest thing to do is communicate with each other. In my job as a police officer I see all kinds of noncommunicating problems, let me tell you. I also run into a lot of temptation from women who are looking for someone to listen or to understand them.

I try to communicate with my wife. I'm blunt and

would like her to be the same. If I do something particular that stimulates her, I'd like to have her let me know about it. I try to let her know what I like, too.

Women don't have enough trust in men. They put wrong values on motives. When I approach a woman to become acquainted with her, she acts like I'm just after sex and that I'm not appreciative of her and her desires, and so forth. I'm automatically a male chauvinist in her eyes, and I don't get to prove myself. If I'm at the local pub and try to meet a woman, she doesn't give me a chance to prove I'm not a chauvinist.

Most women pressure a man to make him want to do something. She doesn't have to pressure him—if he really cares for a woman, there's nothing he wouldn't do. If he's depressed, she has to let him know he's appreciated.

I don't want a woman to put a gun in my back, or a pin in my ass to make me jump. A simple blow in the ear will do.

Some women don't know how to deal with a young man in a depressed situation. Women like to play games or more or less tease.

She should keep things on the same level as when she got into the relationship. If she's tired of the relationship, she should get out and stop playing games. 'Cause I don't like to play games.

In 1977, people don't have as many feelings as they used to—you don't love no woman and beat on her, that's not love. There's too many people getting hurt by love. And women don't understand that men want things to be different, too.

Women don't understand that they confuse men, that men really don't know how to deal with them. A

212

dude tries to be nice and the woman don't appreciate it. If he beats her up she don't really like it, but she stays around. Then she'll cuss him out for being so mean.

•

A lot of women don't understand that men want sex more often than women. I'm 40, have a wife and two girlfriends. If I really like a lady I want to have sex every night—they don't understand that I feel like that when the person is special. My wife says to me, "Do we have to have sex every night?"—but if I'm lying in bed beside a woman, I have no choice.

•

Many women don't understand that men can love, are human beings, and have feelings.

•

I don't think women know that we can hurt. I'm only 20, but I've been in love many times. But each time I hurt differently. The first time I trusted her and she walked out on me. The second time we didn't trust each other. The third lady I wanted badder than anything in the whole wide world, but she didn't want me.

I love all kinds of people, I don't care if they're green—I respect all races and nationalities. I damn sure fall in love easily—like last night I fell in love. She told me today, "Well, Billy, I thought about what you said about us living together, but it probably won't work." But, I'm gonna keep on trying.

12

Coming Together

Men and women want to better understand each other, and they want to be understood. However, besides our biological attributes, each of us carries with us a great deal of cultural baggage—all that we have learned from our environment and our experiences. That men and women have learned different attitudes and modes of behavior and have been taught to value certain ways of acting and personality characteristics is of no surprise. Our upbringing has generally made it difficult for men and women to communicate; the games they play, the sex roles they try to fulfill often impede their relating to each other as human beings. When a man degrades the woman with whom he is having sex, he is not treating her as a human being. When a woman goes out with a man because he owns a spectacular car or because of his money or social status, she is not relating to him as a human being. So as long as we set up courtship rules that dehumanize, we shouldn't be surprised that sexuality becomes a form of barter in this depersonalizing process. Add to this the fact that traditionally we have tried to separate sexuality from life, by either ignoring it or mechanistically approaching it in how-to books as a game-like achievement.

A person who feels healthy, alive, and good about the world is a sexual person. A creative act like writing an article or painting a picture or baking a pie is sensual. Yet our upbringing has made us confine sexuality to the genitals. If two people are feeling sexual, it would be positive if they could learn to enjoy those feelings, without automatically worrying about jumping into bed together (which may not be practical, or morally desirable). Why not learn to enjoy and respond to the sexual vibrations in constructive and affectionate ways? If a person suppresses his or her sensuality in day-to-day life, little wonder that actual physical intercourse is often so difficult and mechanical.

Sensual awakening leads to sexual pleasures. Couples who go to Masters and Johnson to solve sexual problems are encouraged to first enjoy sensual contact together—touching, smells, sights, sounds. Mechanical sex, devoid of sensuality, affection, and communication, is but a shadow of our sexual possibilities.

Most men and women say they do want to understand those of the opposite sex and to improve communication and the quality of their relationships. The first step is to recognize some of the barriers and work to overcome these obstacles. What are some of the differences and some of the similarities between the sexes? To analyze them we must for simplicity's sake overgeneralize, all the while realizing that we all are individuals and have responded to our cultural teachings in unique ways.

SEXUAL FANTASIES

The following is a comparison of the ten most popular sexual fantasies of each sex.

Men's ten most popular fantasies:
1. The nude (or seminude) female body
2. Sex with a woman not previously involved with
3. Past sex experiences
4. Sex with two or more women simultaneously
5. Power and achievement (including being considered an exceptionally good lover)
6. Watching a woman perform in a sexually enticing way
7. Clandestine sex
8. Wife or lover having sexual realtions with another man
9. Sex with a younger woman
10. Sex with woman other than the one having intercourse with at the time

Women's ten most popular fantasies*
1. Sex with a man not previously involved with
2. Past sexual experiences
3. Sensory fantasies
4. Sex with a man other than the one having intercourse with at the time
5. Group sex
6. Being very desirable to men
7. Women's bodies
8. Being coerced into having sex with a man.
9. Sex with more than one man (such as a lineup of men)
10. Sex in a nonsexual place (such as in an elegant restaurant, on a crowded subway, etc.)

While some of the popular sexual fantasies of the two sexes overlap, distinctive differences are apparent. Men have many more fantasies about the nude or seminude female body than do women about the male body. Women are, in fact, more often turned on by

---

* Women's ten most popular fantasies taken from *The Fantasy Files.*

women's bodies than by men's. Such a finding is not surprising in a culture which for centuries has extolled the female body as a stimulus for sexual arousal. Yet, women incorporate the naked or scantily clad male body—especially with an erection—in their fantasies. However, they usually do so by drawing upon experience and not because books and movies of their upbringing have encouraged these supposedly natural imaginings. This does not mean that women, in thinking about other women's bodies, necessarily want to have sexual relations with other women, since most heterosexual women as well are turned on to the female body. They usually make the fantasy heterosexual in nature by thinking of a woman tantalizing men by a striptease or other provocative act.

Men greatly incorporate their striving for power and achievement into their sexual fantasizing. To be the greatest lover around is the height of achievement and a recurrent fantasy. Women don't have as many obvious achievement associations with sexuality, especially achievement in lovemaking. They do, however, have numerous fantasies about being desirable to men. This is especially common during the precoital time.

The difference in these two fantasies illustrates a more general difference in male and female concerns. The woman is more worried about being attractive to a man and hopes the relationship will begin as a result of that attraction. Men also want to attract women, but their biggest concern is being able to perform well once the scenario shifts to the bed, where they can fulfill the woman and sexually succeed.

Both sexes have numerous fantasies of sex with more than one person, but the specifics of these fantasies are quite different, as are the desires to carry them out. Women have frequent fantasies about a lineup of men, each man having sex with her in turn while the other men watch, wanting her. Most women, however, say they don't want to act out this fantasy.

There are strong reasons for the popularity of this

fantasy. The men waiting in line show that they desire the woman, and it is exciting for a woman when a man orgasms inside her. A queue of men assures many of these orgasms in rapid succession. In these lineup fantasies, the woman therefore envisions one potent male after another entering her and orgasming. Few women are turned on by male homosexual activity. The males do not interact sexually with each other; the woman imagines herself, or another woman, as the focal point of sexual interest.

Compare this to the very popular male fantasy of making love to two or more women. The women are not lined up; they are either passively waiting for the male's attention, or, more likely, they are also involved with one another. In this fantasy the man demonstrates his power by fulfilling a number of women. The more women there are, the more arousing the situation, resulting in increased numbers of erections and orgasms. At the same time, the women also interact with each other sexually, for many men are turned on by women making love. Given the "proper" circumstances, a majority of men who have this fantasy would like to enact it.

A striking difference is the frequency of sensory fantasies (bright colors, flowing rivers, shooting stars, sounds, and even smells) that men and women experience during a lovemaking orgasm. Women report many more of these orgasmic fantasies. While these have not reached the "Top Ten" of the male's Fantasy Hit Parade, men are also experiencing them with increased frequency. And like women, men have these sensory fantasies during an emotionally heightened and fulfilling orgasm. As more men let themselves go in sex and communicate more intensely with their partners, they also experience these exciting products of a surrendering and fulfilling encounter with another.

As for the supposed popularity among women of rape and prostitution fantasies, women do have such fantasies, but not to the degree which has been assumed.

In fact, many of these so-called rape fantasies center around the excitement of inescapability rather than enjoyment of being hurt. For that reason I prefer to label them "force" or "coercion" rather than "rape" fantasies, since rape is an act of violence rather than sex. Men also have coercion fantasies; sometimes they want to hurt or coerce the woman and sometimes they want to be forced by a woman to have sex. Also, many of the more traditional men have fantasies about sex with a prostitute.

Men and women both rank among their favorite fantasies depictions of past sex experiences and of sexual encounters with those whom they have not been involved with but are attracted to. There are of course many other fantasy differences and similarities reflecting cultural influence and the ongoing social changes we are all experiencing.

Our fantasies and our sexual turn-ons are inextricable. What are some of the most popular turn-ons for men and women, and, again, where are the differences and similarities?

Most males say they are turned on by specific parts of the female anatomy—breasts, genitals, hair, face, and so forth. But many men say that in addition to a specific part of a woman's anatomy, they are turned on by the total person—the way she carries herself, her personality, her mind.

In recent years women also admit to being attracted to various parts of the male anatomy—thighs, buttocks, legs, hair, face, strong shoulders. Many women are attracted also to the man's personality, his status, and the power he may seem to possess. Intelligence is important in a man. But in general women are most turned on by the whole person—his aura, the combination of qualities, including his dealings with others. If pressed to name one physical characteristic women respond to, it is a man's eyes. Women specify that they are attracted not only to dark or to blue eyes, but to men with "warmth in their eyes," with "humor" reflected in their look, men with "watery, emotional eyes." Although this isn't played up in sex magazines and in macho discussions, men too are drawn to women's eyes and their auras.

"Vibrations" are important to both sexes, and very likely we respond to each other's smells, body chemistry, and many other sensory signals. The "love-at-first-sight" concept can be challenged, but it is true that many men and women size up those of the opposite sex quickly and intuitively. In fact, most of the to-sleep-with or not-to-sleep-with decisions are made by both man and woman during the first ten minutes of their first encounter. A great deal of information and communication goes on between men and women—especially initially. The problem is that most people don't understand what is really happening in this communication because they are responding to subliminal signals, to subconscious cues. In our culture, we focus most of our communication on words, often ignoring the power of body language and the validity of all of our senses.

DIFFERENCES

Men can talk with women about personal subjects more easily than they can with other men. For many this started with their interaction with Mom, which allowed more personal contact and sharing of fears or weaknesses than the time spent with Dad, which often stressed nonemotional interactions, discipline, and "manly" subjects such as sports, cars, or business—all de-emphasizing feelings or communication of hesitancy or fear. Certainly our society encourages such compliance; there are "manly" and "womanly" subjects. Boys and men who have been best friends for years very often do not broach deeply personal subjects, while women who have recently met feel freer to share and explore. So when men want to unload hurt and share very personal feelings or information, they generally feel free1 to let feelings go in the presence of an accepting woman.

It is interesting to watch a male enter a social gathering of women and find he's the only man present. Or have you ever seen a man go into a women's clothing store? He usually manifests great discomfort, makes his purchase as quickly as possible, then exits. In fact the only time most men feel halfway comfortable dealing with a group of women is when there is some defined goal they are trying to reach and the man has formal control of the group. Compare the situation in which a man walks into a social gathering of four women with that of a woman walking into a gathering of four men. Probably the only consistent thing that will happen in each situation is that the group interaction will change tremendously when that fifth person of the opposite sex enters.

There are many reasons for the differences in what happens in these two instances—reasons based on the social role each sex is given, as well as on assumptions regarding their relationship to the opposite sex.

To begin with there is an unwritten assumption among women that they can exchange information about their own and other people's feelings. Men do not share this assumption. Their exchange of information is more logistical and tactical, concentrating on what concretely exists rather than conveying underlying feelings and examining relationships. The means of information delivery are also different. Women allow more seemingly "nonempirical" information into their thought processes, which is one reason women are often stereotyped by men as "mysterious," "illogical," "intuitive," and given the prerogative to "change their minds." Because American men will limit their information exchanges to linear logic, when faced with another pattern of exchange they will feel uncomfortable. Add to this the assumption in our society that a man is supposed to be in control not only of himself but also of the "weaker" sex, and of course the man who walks into a group of women will feel disoriented.

What happens between women when a man walks in? They will often instantly become rivals for the man's attention; he is important. Other women have a lower priority. I remember as a college graduate living in a house with four female roommates we always operated on this assumption, and once in one of our conversations we even articulated it. If we as a group planned an informal outing it wasn't considered rude for one of us to renege at the last moment if indeed that special man wanted to do something else. It was not inconsiderate or disloyal. "Her guy" had priority over everyday activities like some kind of special visitor.

This importance made the group defer; the male interloper became the center of attention. Men don't traditionally hold women in such regard. Even if the woman visitor to a man's group is considered very attractive, there will still remain among the men—even in their competition for her—a bond of camaraderie which probably would not exist in the traditional women's group. Individually and as a unit the men would establish their dominance. If they were previously involved in watching a football game or discussing business they will not change their activity to accommodate her entry. She feels like an intruder in a man's world, but isn't likely to be very concerned or uncomfortable about it because, unlike the male visitor in the women's group, usually she would not be striving to gain dominance or overt control of those around her.

There are, of course, many other explanations behind what might happen in these two situations, but the two differences discussed above in information sharing and personal priorities are important variables in understanding how each of us lives our life and how we relate to someone of the other sex.

As important as exploring the traditional *differences* between the two sexes is an awareness of the many *similarities.* Both men and women want to be appreciated and loved; they have fears, dreams, aspirations. Most want to improve relationships and feel more personal joy and contentment. However, old rules conflict with new roles.

As men and women try to understand and treat each other more as human beings than as sex or status objects, there is inevitable confusion. As frustrating as established ways of relating may be, they at least provided some agreed-upon rules and signals. As the involvement became more intense the woman would press for settling down, getting married, having a monogamous relationship. She, more than he, would want to have some signs along the way to assure her of progression toward their exclusive coupling—frequent calls, weekend evenings together, endearing words culminating in the ultimate "I love you," then emotional commitment, a promise of marriage, and plans for a family.

Today, women enjoying their independence and careers may not be playing this old and trusted game. Men as well may be looking for different rewards in a relationship. The signals change. The professed love may not carry with it future possibilities of a life commitment; or "I love you" may imply a commitment for one person but not for the other.

If a woman is friendly and smiles and talks with a strange man, she might be regarding him as an interesting new acquaintance with whom she would like to share ideas, and if they get along, perhaps share a friendship or romance. If the man is a traditionalist, he might assume this woman's friendliness and informality are a signal that she is a morally "loose" female to be degraded and used. The reverse also happens when a man tries to be friendly with a woman and she becomes offended, thinking that he is not respecting her "and wants only one thing."

Both become annoyed and find their signals and actions have been misinterpreted. Simple situations, such as who pays the check at a meal or who opens the door, can lead to discomfort and misunderstanding, especially when the man and woman are not open with each other or don't take the time to explain what they really have in mind.

Men are trying to be more sensitive to women, and women are trying to become more aggressive and independent. It's not easy. For example, a woman is used to the victim's role and might actually lose interest in the thoughtful male who is treating her as an equal, or she may try to force the relationship back into one in which she is again the victim. All of us resist change; change represents the unknown. The spouse of an alcoholic, for example, might hope fervently that his (her) mate will stop drinking, yet subconsciously will act in such a way as to encourage continuance of that drinking. Often when the alcoholic does indeed stop drinking there is a divorce because the dynamics between the two people have been severely changed. When this happens, when one person changes, the other subconsciously will attempt to recover the past—to restore the old order. The unknown, even if it is a vast improvement, is scary.

Coping with change and trying to break old molds and barriers is indeed frightening and demands the courage about which Rollo May writes in his book *The Courage to Create*. It is not easy to share our feelings when for most of our lives we've been taught not to. It's not easy to change old habits, or to work toward better communication. It's easy to say "let's really talk" but one of the hardest things in the world actually to do.

PAST INTO THE PRESENT

While growing up and in our present lives we are all constantly exploring and readjusting our positions, tottering between subjugation (being dominated by another, being trapped) and rejection (being left alone, abandoned). Generally we try to find a pleasant place somewhere in the middle, avoiding either extreme. In reality most of us grew up in such an environment—neither totally love-bound and secure, nor totally barren of love and security. And most of us did explore and reach out, then retreat to a secure base, to replenish ourselves as it were. And we were raised in a society where boys and girls were treated differently and given different expectations about sexual roles and their individual relationships with parents.

Mothers and Sons

A boy is born into the world and constantly nurtured by the essential female in his life, his mother. She nurses him, she washes him, she kisses and shows him love. All this is necessary to his growth: such love and nurturance are vital even to the physical development of the child.

His very survival depends on her, in fact. As he grows he learns that he must be tough ("boys don't cry") while his sister is more protected. When he goes to school he's surrounded by more female than male teachers, especially in the elementary grades. He doesn't see many male models except a distant, loving, but not overtly affectionate father until his athletic coach comes along to teach him that being a boy is competing in sports and that male affection is shown indirectly in many tough ways—through male camaraderie and competition—not through caressing or touching, as women show affection. The boy tries to form his identity as a male, surmising that he's not supposed to identify totally with his mother because she's not the right sex. Not knowing exactly what to do, he fights not to be subjugated by the "females" around him. Neither does he want to be rejected.

The son struggles with the natural sensuality he feels for his mother. As he grows older, he learns about genital sex, that he must love and respect his mother, that sex with her is an extreme taboo. He attempts to deal with his sexual feelings for her. He may feel guilty or angry as he tries to learn what is the societally correct depository for his sexual urges. Most likely, he will learn at a young age to suppress these feelings and perhaps go through the Freudian stages of sexual development—oral, anal, phallic, homosexual, heterosexual.

He has a great deal to resolve and learn about in growing up, and often his varied feelings about his mother are not understood nor resolved, thereby affecting his involvement with other females. His confusion about his great love and affection for his mother, which are thwarted by taboos that separate him from this source of love and affection, has resulted in the madonna-prostitute categorizing of the other women in his life. Problems of identity and knowing how he should in turn *give* love are exacerbated by the societal teaching that he must not be directly affectionate, warm, or emotional. He carefully separates love from lust—mind from body—and tries to play the macho role. The anxiety built up in early years caused by taboo sexual feelings for his mother may turn into fear of closeness with women in general. His early fear of subjugation and his simultaneous anger at his mother for rejecting him and turning him out too soon to the cold world may make him subconsciously resentful toward his mother; and this unrecognized and unresolved fear, this unrecognized and unresolved anger may then reveal itself when he interacts with other women. Traditional society, in defining his "maleness" for him, tells him to seek out a sex object to release his sexual tensions. But he's not satisfied. Although he can be more explicit and freer sexually in a technical way with a prostitute than with his mother or madonna-wife, this is only half of the picture. He must constantly dichotomize his libidinal urges from his desire to give and receive affection. And so the process goes on. The boy marries a girl like Mom and symbolically acts out part of the relationship with his mother. He's also been taught by this time to be Dad. So he acts with his wife like both son and father (husband), and she in turn acts with him like both daughter and mother (wife), because like him she's living out part of her script with her father and mother and also because these are the models she's seen while growing up that are supposed to show her how to be a "woman."

Fathers and Daughters

The woman learns from her mother that being female consists of being warm, nurturing, and emotional. And because of the predominance of women around her in her early years, she has less difficulty forming her traditionally female identity. But she doesn't quite know how to relate to Dad, and when those sensual/sexual feelings crop up between them she may interpret Dad's reactions to them as rejection. She wants to get close to him, to sit on his lap, to have him touch and kiss her, but he keeps his distance. In fact, many fathers who repress their sexual feelings toward their daughters may become subconsciously anxious as the feelings well up. Some react by physically beating, by physically hurting the daughter. A daughter who has been so abused and/or emotionally rejected by the father will often in later life be attracted to men who treat her in the same manner, partly because she has intuitively perceived the love and sexual anxiety emanating from that outwardly cold father and wants to resolve the past relationship, and partly because Dad is the first important man in her life and she associates his behavior with real manhood. Imitating Mom and interacting with Dad, the traditional woman often learns in growing up that her role is largely one of victim and sacrificer.

Thus, people often tend to try to somehow resolve their past history. Both sexes are still in this subjugation-rejection continuum. A man who is still fighting to be independent of the subjugation of "Mother" will pull away if a woman gets too emotional and serious too fast out of fear the woman is trying to "hook" or change him. And the woman fears most the pain of rejection that she experienced with her father (although paradoxically, since it was mixed with an underlying love, she will also in many ways encourage this very same rejection). So she wants the man with whom she's involved to provide security for her, to give her the wedding ring and eternal promises that he will not reject her. She'll do anything to please him; she's been well taught to be nurturing and affectionate, and he keeps coming back to that love he also wants.

Complicated, yes. And true in many ways for each of us. Yet how do we break out of these traditional rituals and go beyond them? By first recognizing what past scenario we are still involved in and what we really are trying to obtain and resolve through it. If we can recognize our individual script, then we can choose a direction for ourselves. Conscious understanding of our motives and our desires is important. Insights as to why we do certain things and act in certain ways can free us to make some personal choices. Self-understanding can be reached in a variety of ways: through reading and garnering information about our roles and ourselves, through therapy, and/or through sharing very personal parts of ourselves with others and working to understand our individual situations.

So what does this have to do with sexuality? Everything. Sexuality is an integral part of living. As we better understand ourselves—our backgrounds, our feelings, and our goals—we better understand our sexual responses and what for each of us is the natural, enjoyable, and moral way to be a sexual person. We don't have to be unthinking sheep in the sexual revolution. Sexual hunting and pressure to be permissive and sleep with anyone who asks is just as unnatural as the past Victorian repression of sexual expression.

Each person needs to understand more about his or her own potential and upbringing before he or she can better communicate with another. Each person must feel better about him- or herself before truly liking and relating to another. The traditional dedicated mother did not really abandon control. She ruled covertly through guilt. And there is no stronger control over another. There has been a great deal of anger between men and women—mostly because each was not happy with him- or herself and the limited role. As half-persons we each grasped desperately for someone from the opposite sex to make us whole—to finance our life or to raise our children, to faithfully bolster our egos. When this wasn't done to our satisfaction, resentment ensued. We felt resentment, but couldn't bear to be alone, to dismiss our other half. But grasping for someone in loneliness, desperation, or fear of condemnation for not playing agreed-upon, all-American games isn't the best way to live. People are now deciding to learn about what the games are and to choose a personal life-style instead of uncritically accepting a role. And they are helping others do the same.

People are learning. Men and women are learning more humanistic ways of relating based on sincerity and concern for "the other." They are learning to co-ordinate their true feelings with their bodies so sex will stop being a masquerade and can become a part of the person inside. They are becoming whole, sensitive human beings—enhancing their sexuality and their lives.

Appendix

Sex Statistics by Age

Age in Years	On the Average—How Often They Think About Sex	On the Average—How Often They Masturbate	How Many Are Satisfied With Their Sex Life (%)	
			Sat.	Dissat.
12–19	Every 5 minutes	4–5 times a week	53	47
20–29	Every 10 minutes	4–5 times a week	46	54
30–39	Every 15 minutes	3–4 times a week	52	48
40–49	Every half hour	2–3 times a week	33	67
50–59	Every hour	Weekly	30	70
60 and over	Several times a day	Monthly	65	35

Demographic Characteristics of Study Sample: Percentage of Total Subjects (N = 4,062) in Each Division

Area of the Country

Northeast Coast Urban	West Coast Urban	Other Urban Regions	Rural Regions
31.1	24.8	21.5	22.6

The Sexual Sensitivity of the American Male

Marital Status

Single	Married	Separated	Divorced	Widowed
21.1	52.2	7.3	16.6	2.8

Ethnic Background

Caucasian: 51.6 Spanish Surname: 3.9 Asian-American: 1.4
Black: 17.2 Jewish: 24.1 Native American: 1.2
Arab: .6

Sexual Orientation

Heterosexual	Bisexual	Homosexual
87.6	2.1	10.3

Age

12–19 Years	20–29 Years	30–39 Years	40–49 Years	50–59 Years
10.3	21.1	23.2	20.9	16.2

60–69 Years	70 Years and Above
6.5	1.8

Educational Level

Did Not Graduate High School	High School Graduate	Less Than One Year College	One Year College or more	College Graduate	Post Graduate	Advanced Degree
3.2	19.3	4.9	17.8	21.8	11.4	21.6

Demographic Characteristics of Study Sample:
Percentage of Total Subjects (N = 4,062) in Each Division

Religious Training

Catholic	Jewish	Protestant	Other	None
29.8	24.1	36.3	8.6	1.2

Father's Occupation

Blue Collar	White Collar	Not Mentioned
46.3	43.8	9.9

QUESTIONNAIRE

1. *Name* _____ (Optional)
2. *Address* _____ (Optional)
3. *Age Group*
       12–19___   50–59___
       20–29___   60–69___
       30–39___   70 & Over___
       40–49___
4. *Religious Upbringing*
       Catholic___
       Jewish___
       Protestant___
       (If Protestant, what denomination? _____)
       Other_____
       None_____
       Are you still an active member of the afore-mentioned religion?
       Yes___   No___
5. *Marital Status*
       Single___, Married___, Divorced___, Widowed___
       Have you been married more than once?
       Yes___   No___
       (If more than once, how many times? _____)
       Have you ever lived with a woman (outside of marriage)?
       Yes___   No___
6. *Number of Children:* 1___, 2,___, 3___, 4___,
   more than 4___, none___
7. *Occupation*
       Yours _____
       Spouse's (if married) _____
8. *Occupation of Parents*
       Mother _____   Father _____
9. Area of the country where you have spent the majority of your life?
       Northeast coast urban region
       (including Washington, D.C.)—————————

West coast urban region___
Other urban regions___ (Where?_____)
Rural region___ (Where?_____)

10. *Educational Level:*	Yours	Spouse's (if married)
Less than high school	—	—
High school	—	—
Some college (How many years?)	—	—
College graduate	—	—
Some postgraduate	—	—
Advanced degree	—	—

11. *Ethnic Background:*
    Caucasian___
    Black___
    Native American___
    Spanish Surname___
    Jewish___
    Arab___
    Asian___
    Other___

12. How often do you masturbate?
    Several times a day   —
    Daily   —
    Several times a week   —
    Weekly   —
    Monthly   —
    Almost never   —
    Never   —
    I have never experienced masturbation___

13. How often do you think about sex?
    Every two minutes___
    Every five minutes___
    Every ten minutes___
    Every half hour___
    Every hour___
    Several times daily___
    Other___(Approximately
      how often?_____)

14. What books or magazines have you found sexually arousing?

    How have these books or magazines affected your sexual fantasies?

15. What movies have you found sexually arousing?

    How have these movies affected your sexual fantasies?

16. What is your sexual orientation?
    Heterosexual___ Homosexual___ Bisexual___
17. Are you satisfied with your sex life? Yes___ No___
18. I would now like you to describe any sexual fantasies you have had *during* each of the following situations:
    a. Daydreaming
    b. Masturbation
    c. Sexual relations

Please describe each fantasy in complete detail including all *others* involved, human, animals, or objects. Describe this in size, color, type, etc., and include the time and place of the fantasy.

Please do not hesitate to describe any fantasy you have because you might think it's "weird"—you'll probably find it is a very common fantasy. That is the purpose of this study—for men to realize what other men really think about.

In order to be sure we are all interpreting certain terms in the same way, please work in accordance with the following definitions:

fantasy—any daydream, thought, image, or story which comes into your mind (does not include dreams during sleep).

sexual fantasy—any thought, image, or story which is of a sexual nature and/or is sexually arousing to the person having the fantasy.

"daydream" sexual fantasy—sexual fantasy which is

experienced at any time day or night other than during masturbation or sexual relations.

masturbatory sexual fantasy—any sexual fantasy used during masturbation.

sexual fantasy during sexual relations—any sexual fantasy experienced during sexual relations (usually leading up to and during intercourse).

After your description of each fantasy please state: 1. approximately how frequently you have this thought; 2. whether the fantasy ever overlaps into the three situations given above; 3. whether this is a fantasy you experience presently or was it one you used to have; 4. also, please state whether you have ever actually experienced what you are (were) fantasizing—i.e., is this fantasy a replay of a past experience; 5. and finally, for each fantasy, if you have never experienced this fantasy, would you like to, if given the opportunity?

Daydream fantasies

Masturbatory fantasies

Fantasies during sexual relations

Do you usually open or close your eyes during orgasm (during masturbation and/or intercourse)?

Please answer any or all of these questions:

At what times or during what situations do you usually masturbate?

What do you use as an aid in masturbation (i.e., fantasy, picture, etc.)?

Do you use a special technique?

For what reasons do you masturbate?

Do you enjoy masturbating?

Have you ever participated in mutual masturbation?

What does an orgasm feel like? Are there differences in intensity or types?

Do you ejaculate every time you have an orgasm? Do you ever ejaculate without an orgasm?

If you do experience different types of orgasm, what

causes the difference (i.e., situation, time, person, emotional involvement, etc.)?

Do you ever experience fantasies during orgasm?

What do you prefer to do immediately following orgasm (hold your partner, smoke a cigarette, go to sleep, etc.)?

Is it important that you orgasm during a sexual encounter?

Have you ever faked an orgasm? How did you do it?

What were some of your most exciting and/or enjoyable lovemaking experiences?

In what unusual places/settings have you made love?

What was your first sexual experience?

Do you prefer to have sex with older or younger women? Why?

How do you approach a woman for the first time?

Does the size or shape of a woman's vagina affect sex?

How do you make love to a woman? Is there a pattern, a consistent technique you mostly use?

How do you feel about women's orgasms? Do you ever wonder what an orgasm feels like to a woman? Do you know when the woman you are with has one?

What does a vagina feel like?

Do you like the women to be active during lovemaking —to thrust and move?

Do you prefer oral or genital sex?

Do you prefer a certain way or position to attain orgasm during intercourse?

What do you like your partner to do during lovemaking?

Are there special things you like your partner to do while giving you oral sex?

Is it important in sexual relations whether a man is circumcised or not?

What type of contraception do you prefer?

How does alcohol or marijuana affect your sex life?

In general, what don't women understand about men, or specifically, what don't women you know understand about you?

Please comment on any other issues about sexuality

which may not have been covered in these questions which may interest you and which you feel should be discussed in a study such as this.

(If more room is needed, use back of pages or insert more paper. If you mail this questionnaire back, please tear off page 1 and the bottom half of page 4, the directions, in order to stay within the 15¢ postage weight limitation.) PLEASE TRY TO RETURN QUESTIONNAIRE WITHIN THREE DAYS. THANK YOU.

BIBLIOGRAPHY

Beach, Frank A. *Human Sexuality in Four Perspectives.* Baltimore and London: Johns Hopkins University Press, 1976.

Beit-Hallahmi, John. "Sexual and Aggressive Fantasies in Violent and Non-Violent Prison Inmates," *Journal of Personality Assessment,* XXXV (August, 1970), 326–330.

Belliveau, Fred, and Lin Richter. *Understanding Human Sexual Inadequacy.* New York: Bantam, 1970.

Bierstedt, Robert. *The Social Order.* New York: McGraw-Hill, 1970.

Brecher, Edward M. *The Sex Researchers.* Boston: Little, Brown, 1969.

Cameron, Paul. "Answers to Questions," *Sexual Behavior,* II, 3 (March 1972), 7.

Davis, Keith. "Sex on the campus: Is there a revolution?" *Medical Aspects of Human Sexuality,* 1971, 5, 128–142.

Ellis, Albert. *An Impolite Interview with Albert Ellis.* New York Institute for Rational Living, 1960.

———. *The Sensuous Person.* New York: New American Press, 1972.

———. *Sex and the Liberated Man.* New Jersey: Lyle Stuart, Inc., 1976.

————, and Albert Abarbanel, eds. *The Encyclopedia of Sexual Behavior*. New York: Jason Aronson, Inc., 1973.

Fried, Christopher. "Icarianism, Masochism, and Sex Differences in Fantasy," *Journal of Personality Assessment*, XXXV, I (February, 1971).

Freud, Sigmund. "Beyond the Pleasure Principle." *The Standard Edition of the Complete Psychological Works of Sigmund Freud*, vol. XVIII, trans. and ed. James Strachey. London: Hogarth Press and the Institute of Psychoanalysis, 1953.

————. *Character and Anal Eroticism*. New York: Norton Library Press, 1925.

————. *Collected Papers*, vol. II, trans. and ed. Joan Rivera. London: Institute of Psychoanalysis, 1924–1925.

————. *Delusion and Dream*, ed. Philip Rieff. New York: Beacon Press, 1956.

————. *The Ego and the Id*. London: Hogarth Press, 1927.

————. "Formulations of the Two Principles of Mental Functioning," *The Standard Edition of the Complete Psychological Works of Sigmund Freud*, vol. XII, trans. and ed. James Strachey. London: Hogarth Press and the Institute of Psychoanalysis, 1958.

————. "The Leonardo da Vinci and a Memory of His Childhood," *The Standard Edition of the Complete Psychological Works of Sigmund Freud*, vol. XI, trans. and ed. James Strachey. London: Hogarth Press and the Institute of Psychoanalysis, 1957.

Gagnon, John H. *Human Sexualities*. Glenview, Ill.: Scott, Foresman and Co., 1977.

Greenwald, Harold, and Ruth Greenwald. *The Sex-Life Letters*. New York: Bantam Books, 1973.

————, and Natalie Shainess. "Debate: Are Fantasies During Sexual Relations a Sign of Difficulty?" *Sexual Behavior*, 1, 2 (May, 1971), 50–54.

Guerney, Bernard G., Jr. *Relationship Enhancement*. San Francisco: Jossey-Bass Publishers, 1977.

Bibliography

Hartmann, Heinz. *Ego Psychology and the Problem of Adaptation,* trans. David Rappaport. New York: Columbia University Press, 1965.

Hilgard, Ernest R. *Introduction to Psychology.* 3d ed. New York: Harcourt, Brace and World, 1962.

Horney, Karen. *New Ways in Psychoanalysis.* New York: Norton and Company, 1939.

Hunt, Morton. *The Affair.* New York: World Publishing, 1969.

————. *Sexual Behavior in the 1970s.* Chicago: Playboy Press, 1974.

Jessor, Shirley, and Richard Jessor. "Transition from virginity to nonvirginity among youth: A social psychological study over time." *Developmental Psychology,* 1975, 11, 473–484.

Jung, Carl. *Contributions to Analytical Psychology.* London: Truler, 1928.

————. *Modern Man in Search of a Soul,* trans. W. S. Dell and Cary I. Baynes. New York: Harcourt Brace, 1933.

Kaplan, Helen S. *The New Sex Therapy.* New York: Quadrangle/The New York Times Book Co., 1974.

————. *The New Sex Therapy.* New York: Brunner/Mazel, Inc., 1974.

————, and Clifford J. Sager. "Sexual patterns at different ages." *Medical Aspects of Human Sexuality,* June 1971, 5, 10 ff.

Kinsey, Alfred C., Wardell Pomeroy, and Clyde Martin. *Sexual Behavior in the Human Male.* Philadelphia and London: W. B. Saunders Company, 1948.

Krafft-Ebing, Richard von. *Psychopathic Sexuality.* London: Cambridge Press, 1893.

————. *Psychopathia Sexualis.* New York: G. P. Putnam's Sons, 1965.

Kronhausen, P., and E. Kronhausen. *Erotic Fantasies: A Study of the Sexual Imagination.* New York: Grove Press, 1969.

La Piere, Richard T. *Social Change.* New York: McGraw-Hill Book Company, 1965.

Lample de Groot, Jeanne. *The Development of the Mind.* London: Norton Press, 1965.

Langer, Susanne K. *Philosophy in a New Key.* New York: The New American Library, 1951.

Lilly, John C. "Mental Effects of Reduction of Ordinary Levels of Physical Stimuli on Healthy Persons," *Psychiatric Research Report V* (1956), 1–9.

Lorenz, Konrad. *On Aggression.* New York: Harcourt, Brace and World, Inc., 1966.

Marcus, Irwin, and John J. Francis, eds. *Masturbation from Infancy to Senescence.* New York: International Universities Press, Inc., 1975.

Marris, Peter. *Loss and Change.* New York: Pantheon Books, Inc., 1974.

Maslow, A. H. "Self Esteem (Dominance Feeling) and Sexuality in Women," *Journal of Social Psychology* XVI (1942), 259–264.

————. "Critique and Discussion: Part I," *Sex Research: New Developments,* ed. J. Money. New York: Holt, Rinehart and Winston, 1965, 135–143.

————. *Toward a Psychology of Being.* New York: Van Nostrand Reinhold Company, 1968.

————, H. H. Rand, and S. Newman. "Some Parallels Between the Dominance and Sexual Behavior of Monkeys and the Fantasies of Psychoanalytic Patients," *Journal of Nervous and Mental Disease* CXXXI (1960), 202–212.

Masters, W. H., and V. E. Johnson. *Human Sexual Inadequacy.* Boston: Little, Brown & Co., 1970.

————. *Human Sexual Response.* Boston: Little, Brown & Co., 1966.

————, in association with Robert J. Levin. *The Pleasure Bond.* Boston: Little, Brown & Co., 1974.

May, Robert, "Fantasy Differences in Men and Women," *Psychology Today,* LXIX (April, 1968), 42–45.

May, Rollo. *The Courage to Create.* New York: W. W. Norton and Company, 1975.

Newman, Gustave, and Claude R. Nichols. "Sexual activities and attitudes in older persons." In Nathaniel N. Wagner, ed., *Perspectives on Human Sexuality*. New York: Behavioral Publications, Inc., 1974, 501–508.

Perls, Fredrich S. *Ego, Hunger, and Aggression*. New York: Random House, 1969.

Playboy Survey: "Sexual Behavior in the 1970's," October 1973, pp. 84–88; and November 1973, pp. 74–75.

Proctor, E. B., N. N. Wagner, and Julius C. Butler. "The differentiation of male and female orgasm: an experimental study." In Nathaniel N. Wagner, ed., *Perspectives on Human Sexuality*. New York: Behavioral Publications, Inc., 1974, 115–132.

Reich, Wilhelm. *Character Analysis*. 3d ed. New York: Noonday, 1949.

Reik, T. *Of Love and Lust: On the Psychoanalysis of Romantic and Sexual Emotions*. New York: Bantam, 1967.

Rosen, Linda. "The experience of orgasm: His and hers." *Advisor: The Journal of Human Sexuality,* April 1977, II, 30–35.

Rubin, Isadore. *Sexual Life after Sixty*. New York: Basic Books, 1965.

Sanford, Nevitt, et al. "Physique, Personality, and Scholarship," *Psychiatry,* VII (1944), 282.

Schaefer, Leah Cahan. "Sexual Experiences and Reactions of a Group of Thirty Women as Told to a Female Psychotherapist." Report of an Ed.D. Doctoral Project. New York: Teachers College, Columbia University, 1964.

———. *Women and Sex*. New York: Pantheon Books, 1973.

Shanor, Karen I., *Social Variables of Women's Sexual Fantasies*. Unpublished dissertation, United States International University, San Diego, 1974.

———. *The Fantasy Files*. New York: Dial Press, 1977.

Singer, J. L. *Daydreaming: An Introduction to the Ex-*

perimental Study of Inner Experience. New York: Random House, 1966.

Slattery, William J. *The Erotic Imagination.* Chicago: Henry Regnery Company, 1975.

Sorensen, Robert C. *Adolescent Sexuality in Contemporary America.* New York: World Publishing, 1973.

Symonds, Percival Mallon. *The Dynamics of Human Adjustment.* New York: Appleton-Century Company, 1946.

Tavris, Carol. "Good news about sex." *New York,* December 6, 1976, 9, 51–57.

————. "Men and women report their views on masculinity," *Psychology Today,* January 1977, 10, 35–42, 82.

Weinberg, Martin S., ed. *Sex Research: Studies from the Kinsey Institute.* New York: Oxford University Press, 1976.

Wetzsteon, Ross. "Do men want to be sex objects?" *Village Voice,* November 1, 1976, 11–13.